Soul-Kissed

Soul-Kissed

The Experience of Bliss in Everyday Life

Ann Tremaine Linthorst

A Crossroad Book
The Crossroad Publishing Company
New York

1996

The Crossroad Publishing Company
370 Lexington Avenue, New York, NY 10017

Printed in the United States of America

Library of Congress Cataloging-in-Publication Data

Linthorst, Ann.
    Soul-kissed : the experience of bliss in everyday life / Ann
Tremaine Linthorst.
      p. cm.
    Includes bibliographical references.
    ISBN 0-8245-1492-0 (pbk.)
    1. Ecstasy. 2. Soul. 3. Linthorst, Ann.   I. Title.
BL626.L56 1996
291.4–dc20
                                          95-51045
                                           CIP

For the Marys:

> *. . . Mother of Jesus*
> *. . . Mother of Science*
> *. . . Mother of Ann*

and the Johns:

> *. . . Beloved Disciple*
> *. . . Beloved Teacher*
> *. . . Beloved Husband*

> *. . . Soul-Seers, All*

Thank you very much!
Thank you very much!
Thank you very much!

Contents

Acknowledgments

Personal thanks to Michael Leach for proving that the encouragement and guidance of writers is not a thing of the past, at least at Crossroad, and to John Eagleson for his attentive and beautiful work.

Thanks to the following for permission to reprint excerpts:

To Michael Beard, president of Macalester Park Publishing Co., for permission to reprint excerpts from the 1947 publication *Twenty Minutes of Reality*.

To the Christian Science Publishing Society for permission to quote from Irving Tomlinson's book *Twelve Years with Mary Baker Eddy*.

To HarperCollins Publishers for permission to quote from Raynor C. Johnson's book *Watcher on the Hills*.

To John White, literary agent for Nona Coxhead, for permission to quote from *The Relevance of Bliss* (St. Martin's Press, 1985).

To Doubleday and Co., for permission to quote from *The Three Pillars of Zen* by Philip Kapleau.

Introit

This book is about finding and living out from Soul, that center within each of us where we are *aware* of being made in the image and likeness of God. Soul is a reservoir of wholeness that embraces and heals our brokenness, a clarity of values that unerringly guides us to the good, a blessedness that cares for us in the details of daily experience and kisses us with glimpses of bliss.

Does that sound too good to be true? Would you settle for just a little less hassle and a little more money? Then this book is not for you. Soul is very subtle and seems very shy amid the blare of the demanding and conflicting voices of human selfhood. Bliss stays veiled in the presence of ego. We must care greatly about Soul before we will be able to notice Its care for us. Soul, with Its blissful seeing, cannot be commanded, yet neither does It establish Itself in our experience unbidden.

This book is for those who want to move beyond the experience of life as problem-solving. Daily life seems, to most people, to be an endless series of difficulties to be managed, if not overcome. But it is not that to Soul. Living from our Soul center, life becomes the ongoing expression of spiritual qualities. Our daily experience becomes a palette colored with spiritual hues. Nothing dramatic. Just more peace, more harmony, more love and beauty. More trips to the ice cream store than to the doctor. More walks in nature than in jostling mobs of people. More affectionate touches given and received. More smiles, fewer frowns.

All of the above changes, and many more, have taken place in my own experience as I have come to realize that Soul, rather than personhood, is my name and my nature. Nothing beats spiritual Self-discovery when it comes to finding the sense of worth and fulfillment for which everyone longs. Personhood is actually a misconception of the truth of our being. Trying to live on the basis of such a misconception of our identity prevents us from claiming the things that rightly belong to us.

We would not go on an ocean cruise and settle for a cot, and a job, in the engine room. We would expect, even demand, a comfortable stateroom with all the amenities. Yet many people labor through their human lives, sweating and complaining, never realizing that their cause for complaint is legitimate. They have been fooled into accepting a mistaken placement. Life is not asking anybody to settle for engine room accommodations. A stateroom awaits us all. But it must be claimed.

In this book, I will share my own Soul pilgrimage and many of the resources that are helping me along the way. Especially I want to share bliss reports and a way to use them that can operate, increasingly, to open our eyes to the universe of Soul. These reports tell of what are usually called mystical experiences. Mystical, or bliss, experiences are direct realizations of divine consciousness and Life. They reveal what Soul is seeing, which is what divine Life is being. Such realizations occur when the human sense of identity, which I refer to as ego, momentarily drops away. What reveals itself when that personal ego lens disappears is not only a vision of universal good, but the capacity in us that sees that vision. *The discovery of what Soul sees is also the discovery of Soul as the identity of our seeing.*

For me, repeated immersion in bliss testimonies has done more than any other spiritual practice to heighten my Soul awareness and enable me to claim my Soul heritage. In order to profit from the study of bliss reports, however, it's important to know how to read them. If such experiences are unknown to us, then such a report may seem like a description of a very beautiful place to which we have never been. We will read either as interested travelers who hope, someday, to visit that land. Or we will read as envious stay-at-homes, who feel stuck in a less beautiful environment. Then we may resent that someone else has gotten to go to some gorgeous place that we don't know how to get to.

In the beginning, my reading was tinged with envy, yet I was so enthralled by the visions that I kept being drawn back to them, again and again. I found that I could let myself be taken into the loveliness of the scene if I read it as a revelation of the actual nature of things, which is as true for me as for the seer. As I cherished and savored the images in the reports, I began to taste the flavor of spiritual Life. More and more, I felt included in, rather than excluded from, the reported goodness. Understood to be reports from our own Soul center, bliss reports give us the experience of being fed, from within, with heavenly manna.

The aim of this book is the blissification of each reader's seeing. Yes, blissification: a refinement of seeing that is enlightening, healing, and harmonizing. While we may never have dramatic visions such as those reported in this book, we can all come to a heightened awareness of the qualities of good already present in our experience. We can all have moments of knowing Soul's nurturing presence and care, kissing the core of our being with the sweetness and warmth of divine Love.

CHAPTER 1

Soul Revelation

Why art thou cast down, O my soul? and why art thou disquieted within me? hope thou in God: For I shall yet praise him, who is the health of my countenance.

—PSALM 43:5

Unless one is born from above, he cannot see the kingdom of God.... That which is born of the flesh is flesh, and that which is born of the Spirit is spirit.

—JESUS (JOHN 3:3, 6, RSV)

Soul Quest

What is this "soul" that has captured the best-seller charts in our day? I am going to hazard a definition that, I think, hints at what is so important to us. It is: *sacred identity*. Soul is each individual's sense of being more than what we know of ourselves humanly and of being better than our human self often can actualize. This "more and better" sense of ourselves points to our sacred identity, made "in the image and likeness of God."

I think that the current surge of interest in soul points to a recognition that we must find our security and well-being within. The word "soul" awakens a voice within us that has been too long ignored or relegated to the bottom of our mental agendas. The attempt to find wholeness and satisfaction, safety and abundance, by looking to others is bankrupting, big-time, right in our faces. We are barraged with evidences of that bankruptcy via every form of national and global communications, every moment. Even while we rail at the inability of elected officials, police, the media, and health care professionals to take care of us properly, there is an increasing recognition that the solution to our predicament lies within, or nowhere at all. We must find spiritual identity and dominion, or we will be swamped by the demons, within and without, that we seem helpless to control.

And so we quest for soul. The quest arises not because soul is absent, but because it is present. As our external dependencies fail us, the fact of soul identity makes itself known to us. Books about soul, spiritual values, life after death, and consciousness factors in healing represent the truth of our sacred identity revealing itself more clearly as we become more willing to look beyond self for our salvation.

In this book, I make a clear distinction between our *humanness* and our *Soulness*. In traditional Judeo-Christian thinking, this has not been the case. The sense in the Old Testament, especially in the Psalms, is of soul being the equivalent of "heart," that is, the center of our deepest feelings. But the soul can be "cast down" and must "hope" in God. In this usage, soul keeps the sense of being separate from God, and from other souls as well. It is expressive of human emotions and is, like a human being, "in process."

I think that the power of Soul is undermined by seeing it as some sort of blend of human and divine characteristics. I capitalize the word "Soul" to indicate Its absolute, universal nature, which transcends separate identity. For myself, transformation of feelings and experience has occurred as I have come to see Soul as that place within where the fullness of pure divine Life floods into expression. It appears, first, as awareness, and then that awareness takes form as experience. Soul does not separate me from others, because Soul is a state of consciousness within which all sense of separation from the one Life dissolves.

In contrast, human identity is the sense of personhood, which is established by separation, location, and limitation. Ask yourself who you are, and the details that come to mind will all be statements of location and limitation: "I am male or female, born there, to that father and mother, living here, in this house, with these people, doing this, having that." This kind of self-identification, which I call "ego" throughout the book, automatically excludes all other possibilities. Being here we cannot be anywhere else. Having what we have and doing what we do means that we don't have or do other things. Personal identity is determined precisely by separation, location, and distinction from others. I know that I am Ann, and not Mary or George, by the differences that distinguish and separate us.

Ego Seeing versus Soul Seeing

The distinction between Soul and ego enables us to understand how consciousness, or awareness — I use the terms interchangeably — operates. Then we can begin to exercise dominion over our thinking and feelings. Soul, our sacred identity, operates as our spiritual subjectivity, that is, as spiritual awareness. It shows us a different view of things than does the ego, our material, personal subjectivity. *There are, so to speak, "ego eyes" and "Soul eyes" and, because they see things differently, they see different things.* Jesus said to his disciples, "Blessed are the eyes which see the things that ye see," suggesting that many people, even "prophets and kings," were not able to see in that way (Luke 10:23–24).

Ego eyes see from the standpoint of the belief that reality is essentially material and personal. Soul eyes see from the standpoint of the understanding that reality is essentially spiritual and universal. Each standpoint sees what that premise about reality allows to be seen. Soul sees universal, quality Life, and that seeing is bliss. Ego cannot see beyond its lens of material, personal beliefs. Since this is so, we may feel that testimonies of bliss experiences cannot reach or help us in our personal experience. However, bliss reports confirm to us the essential truthfulness of the premise that reality is actually spiritual and universal. We can, therefore, reason from that premise even when ego is insisting on its limited seeing. This is not Pollyanna thinking, which represses the evidence of the senses. This is being able to see and reason beyond the evidence of the senses.

The distinction between ego eyes and Soul eyes can, perhaps, best be illustrated by an experience I had many years ago. Our second son, Erik, did not sleep through the night for many months after his birth. Since sleep was very important to me, this became a time of crisis. A future of endless nights, walking the floor with a crying baby, loomed before me. I began to wonder if I would survive his infancy.

One night Erik was fussing and fussing, as if he were uncomfortable or in pain. After taking every conceivable step to make him comfortable, without seeming to relieve the problem, I was beginning to feel desperate. Just then a sentence that I had recently read in a spiritual periodical came to mind. It said something like: "The belief of a child in pain reveals a lack of understanding of the nature of divine Love." A sense of abject ignorance filled me, and I said out loud, "Oh, Eriky, we just don't know enough about Love." I felt like a total dunce in the school of love. A sense of the inadequacy of my understanding silenced and humbled me. Eventually, the baby slept and I went back to bed.

The next day, after putting the boys down for their naps, I felt a sudden urgency to get outdoors. Walking out into our backyard, I found that all the green, growing things spoke to me of Love. Everywhere I looked, Love seemed to be throbbing through the trees and bushes and flowers. The whole garden was alive with a dynamic energy of Love, which left me stunned and filled with wonder. I remember consciously noting that the sense was of some inner veil having dropped, revealing the always-present nature of things, rather than of something having happened "out there" to change things. The thought kept repeating itself: "You have to be blind not to see this." Love's presence seemed so obvious, so inescapably in evidence, that it was hard to believe I had not noticed it before.

This was my first bliss experience and the clearest I have ever had. Though the vividness of this vision faded quickly, the revelation of Love as a dynamic, omnipresent energy has been a guidepost in my understanding ever since. Moreover, it provided a first-hand experience of a spontaneous shift from ego eyes to Soul eyes. The statement pointing to divine Love came to mind as Soul eyes replaced ego eyes. Soul seeing brought about a spontaneous recognition of the inadequacy of the ego viewpoint: "We just don't know enough about Love." That realization was, at the same time, the acknowledgement of a vastly larger Love, the awareness of which was the solution to the claims of a baby in pain and a harassed mother. The next morning, Soul eyes revealed the kingdom of Love in my very own backyard.

The Soul Yardstick

Soul helps us see through, and not settle for, the inadequate and depriving beliefs about ourselves and others and life into which we were all born. We must have a standard apart from the ego lens if we are to escape its poverty and imprisonment. While Soul is something we can discover only individually, within, we can clearly define the nature of Soul and Its seeing with the help of bliss reports. Then we have a fixed and reliable yardstick with which to distinguish the misconceptions of the human lens from the substance of divine Life.

The Soul yardstick is *spiritual quality.* As we shall increasingly discover throughout this book, Soul sees quality Life. It sees a wholeness of love, harmony, beauty, vitality, intelligence, innocence, purity, and all the other qualities of Spirit. Qualities, we may notice, are nondimensional, that is, not material, therefore not located, and consequently they are universal. Consciousness that is quality-oriented is lifted out of the locatedness of human sense. The more we pay attention to quality, the more we are living and seeing out from Soul. The more we pay attention to persons, places, and things as separate, substantial realities, the more the ego lens is running our show.

For our own well-being, it is important to understand that the more emphasis there is on material and personal levels of thought, the less we will be aware of quality Life. The principle of consciousness involved here was stated by Jesus as "You cannot serve two masters... you cannot serve God and mammon." This is not a religious injunction but a law of consciousness.

The popular media invite our preoccupation with the lowest, grossest levels of the ego lens. The level of seeing that dominates popular entertainment and news reports focuses on bodies and the most grotesque bodily and personal experiences. As a nation, we are beginning to rebel against the garbage bombardment of daily media fare and seek a healthier mental diet. But most of us are relatively unfamiliar, and even uncomfortable, with quality consciousness. It may seem vague and unstructured. This points to the great value of studying reports of quality awareness, so that we begin to feel at home with Soul's sense of things. Soul seeing does not take away the tangibility of our world. It infuses it with light and warmth. Soul sense is the sunlight of our lives.

Recognizing Soul

Most of us, when we attempt to look within, run into personal feel-ings, thoughts, memories, and fantasies. We don't know how to get beyond the barrier of the personal ego lens, with its mental and emo-tional stuff. I spent five and a half years in analytical psychotherapy without getting even a whiff of Soul. But many years later, I made a discovery that changed my sense of what lies "within" me.

My discovery came quite spontaneously one day, as I took my daily walk in a park. Looking at a familiar scene, the thought came, "How beautiful!" Then a question: "How do I know that that is beauti-ful?" The answer came: "It must be beauty itself, seeing itself." And I thought, then, of the times I read a statement and find myself men-tally exclaiming, "How true!" Again the question raised itself: "How do I know it is true?" Again the reply: "It must be truth itself, see-ing itself." I pondered how these moments are clearly recognitions — re-cognitions — implying that something has already been cognized, or known. Otherwise, instead of finding the thought "How beautiful" or "How true" springing to mind, I could only peer blankly, thinking, "What is this?" or I would simply pass it by unseen.

This discovery gave me a wonderful sense that spiritual qualities, such as beauty and truth, are already present in and as my conscious-ness. Not only is "beauty in the eye of the beholder," but also harmony, truth, order, innocence, purity, and all the other qualities of the spir-itual realm. This was a beginning recognition — that word, again — of Soul as my identity and of Soul seeing taking place all the time, even when ego seems to obscure it. This recognition has very much enhanced my appreciation of bliss reports.

Bliss testimonies teach us how to Soul-see rather than ego-see be-cause they show us how to whole-see rather than parts-see. Nothing written from a human standpoint can communicate the perception of wholeness in the way that bliss reports consistently do. I call these re-ports "Soul maps" because they provide us with ways of reading our everyday experience so that we can increasingly see and identify, right here, right now, the voice and vision of Soul. Then we notice, more and more, the moments of simple peace, joy, gratitude, playfulness, and satisfaction that are our common fare but that personal sense is likely to dismiss in its pursuit of the humanly exciting and dramatic.

Twenty Minutes of Reality

By far the most influential bliss testimony in my experience is the one originally published in the *Atlantic Monthly* magazine in 1916 under the title, "Twenty Minutes of Reality."[1] In this one report we find a useful discussion of the conditions for such a Soul revelation, as well as a very vivid and clarifying report of and discussion about the nature of the divine Life that only Soul sees.

The article was published anonymously, and only in subsequent reprintings did the author, Margaret Prescott Montague, attach her name to it. Miss Montague, a known writer of both fiction and non-fiction in her day, had been rushed to a hospital for surgery on a tumor, which turned out to be benign. She was recovering in a Massachusetts hospital when, on a "dingy" March day, her bed was pushed out into an open bay. She was contemplating the gray, melting snow and the "colorless little city sparrows" when,

> ... my eyes were opened, and for the first time in all my life I caught a glimpse of the ecstatic beauty of reality.

A heightened sense of beauty is characteristic of bliss testimonies and one of the features that is most delightful to me. In the current fictionalized presentation of consciousness issues *The Celestine Prophecy*, James Redfield suggests that the cultivation of a sense of beauty may usher consciousness into a discernment of the underlying field of divine energy.[2] We know that seeing beauty doesn't make our perception any less tangible but, in fact, greatly enhances our appreciation of what we are seeing. This helps us realize that we have nothing to fear from becoming quality-oriented rather than matter-oriented in our thinking. Indeed, Jesus, in the remarks quoted at the beginning of the chapter, states unequivocally that a shift from the focus of "the flesh" to that of Spirit is required in order to see "the kingdom of God."

Shift of Vision, Not Externals

From a human point of view, change means a shift in the externals. In the following passage, Montague emphasizes that the change is not in things but in the way "the usual things" are seen. Soul eyes discern not just beauty, but "the beauty of holiness," that is, beauty as an aspect of the wholeness of universal Life. Each "thing" is seen, not in its separate-thingness, but as a transparency to the wholeness of quality Life.

> I cannot now recall whether the revelation came suddenly or gradually; I only remember finding myself in the very midst of those wonderful moments, beholding life for the first time in all its young intoxication of loveliness, in its unspeakable joy, beauty, and importance....I saw no new thing, but I saw all the usual things in a miraculous new light — in what I believe is their true light. I saw for the first time how wildly beautiful and joyous, beyond any words of mine to describe, is the whole of life. Every human being moving across that porch, every sparrow that flew, every branch tossing in the wind, was caught in and was part of the whole mad ecstasy of loveliness, of joy, of importance, of intoxication of life.

As you read, take time to relish every adjective and noun, sinking into the quality flavor of the vision. This practice works wonders in cultivating quality sense. Montague continues,

> It was not that for a few keyed-up moments I *imagined* all existence as beautiful, but that my inner vision was cleared to the truth so that I *saw* the actual loveliness which is always there, but which we so rarely perceive; and I knew that every man, woman, bird, and tree, every living thing before me, was extravagantly beautiful, and extravagantly important. And as I beheld, my heart melted out of me in a rapture of love and delight. A nurse was walking past; the wind caught a strand of her hair and blew it out in a momentary gleam of sunshine, and never in my life before had I seen how beautiful beyond all belief is a woman's hair. Nor had I ever guessed how marvelous it is for a human being to walk. As for the internes in their white suits, I had never realized before the whiteness of white linen; but much more than that, I had never so much as dreamed of the mad beauty of young manhood. A little sparrow chirped and flew to a nearby branch, and I honestly

believe that only "the morning stars singing together, and the sons of God shouting for joy" can in the least express the ecstasy of a bird's flight.

The Key, and Three Steps, to Soul Seeing

"The actual loveliness which is always there, but which we so rarely perceive." In this sentence, Montague gives us, not as a concept but as something experienced, a key to Soul seeing: *Soul's seeing is what is always taking place no matter what our human sense of things may be declaring at any given moment.* With this key, we may substantially increase our capacity to see from and as Soul, even though we may never have a moment of such spontaneous liberation as hers.

One very practical way of reminding ourselves of Soul's presence and operation is to think about the room we are sitting in at the moment. Right now, that room is filled with music. Symphonies and rock groups are playing, choirs and soloists singing, every conceivable variety of music is being performed. If we have a radio and if it is plugged in, tuned to the proper frequency, and turned on, we will be able to hear the music. If not, then we will hear nothing and will think that the room is empty of music.

Likewise, to see and experience the love, harmony, beauty, intelligence, creativity, and vitality of Life, we will need to have our receiver, which is consciousness, (1) plugged in, (2) tuned to the right frequency, and (3) turned on.

(1) We plug in by acknowledging Soul's presence and operation as our own seeing, here and now, no matter what the ego reports. (2) Understanding that it is a quality frequency, we tune in by directing our attention to quality. We deliberately lay aside the sensual/emotional frequency of perception. This is akin to Jesus' advice to "enter into our closet and shut the door" when we pray. (3) We celebrate and enjoy the universal, quality viewpoint in whatever forms may be most meaningful to us. We let Soul "turn us on" instead of ego, using meditation, artistic activities, nature walks — whatever best helps us to get beyond the confines of ego seeing.

Stretching Consciousness

I cannot overstate the value and importance of a practice of stretching one's consciousness by grateful, devoted immersion in the vision of Soul reports. Ask yourself: How many times a day, normally, does my thought even touch upon such words/ideas as "loveliness, beauty, ecstasy, joy," the "extravagant importance" of "every living thing" and so on? Most of us, I think, would find that such qualities, values, and images rarely register in the midst of the repetitive thought and fantasy patterns with which our minds are normally filled.

Consciousness is where God is; God's kingdom is a consciousness kingdom. Allowing our thinking to be fogged up with images from the "sea of mental garbage" makes no sense. A devoted Christian friend recently confessed her anger at the fact that God reveals Himself so rarely, when our need for His revelations is so great. But God's revelation is continuous. What is rare is an ability and willingness to look beyond the captivating, self-centered dramas of personal sense. We must honor quality Life or we will not see it. We honor it by loving to notice the good that is already in our experience and by longing to see more evidence of its presence.

Nothing that any ego can dream up for itself can begin to approximate in quality the wonders of God's spiritual universe. Laying aside the ego's insistences, fantasies, and even personal prayers, daily, in order to frolic in transpersonal visions of bliss, is a spiritual exercise of not only great value but of unspeakable joy as well. How I have enjoyed seeing in my young adult sons "the mad beauty of young manhood" to which Montague's report awakened me. How much more I enjoy watching the birds outside my window and the tree branches "tossing in the wind" now that I see them as illustrations of "the whole mad ecstasy of loveliness, of joy, of importance, of intoxication of life." For Valentine's Day, my husband bought me a bird feeder to hang outside my window. Each morning he puts seed in it, and the delighted dances of the feeding birds enhance my spiritual study time.

Montague pauses to summarize her experience:

> Once out of all the gray days of my life I have looked into the heart of reality; I have witnessed the truth; I have seen life as it really is — ravishingly, ecstatically, madly beautiful, and filled

to overflowing with a wild joy, and a value unspeakable. For those glorified moments I was in love with every living thing before me — the trees in the wind, the little birds flying, the nurses, the internes, the people who came and went. There was nothing that was alive that was not a miracle. Just to be alive was in itself a miracle. My very soul flowed out of me in a great joy.

Here, as in the beginning, the juxtaposition of "gray" with the reported beauty of reality heightens our sense of the shift, like a black-and-white movie that suddenly explodes into vivid technicolor. And then the thundering waterfall of descriptive words: "ravishingly, ecstatically, madly beautiful, and filled to overflowing with a wild joy and a value unspeakable." All three of the initial adjectives point to the effect in consciousness of the vision: the mind is ravished, driven crazy with ecstasy. Nothing ordinary, pedestrian, or boring here! The joy of the experience is wild; consciousness floods, overflows, and the sense of value surpasses language. Such a description goes a long way toward effecting that very change in the consciousness of the reader if it is lovingly, attentively read.

Since I first heard this passage quoted, I have been a grateful devotee of this definition of Life "as it really is": *ravishingly, ecstatically, madly beautiful, and filled to overflowing with a wild joy, and a value unspeakable.* I consider it a priceless gift of grace and goodness just to have encountered this description of Life. I have lived with and cherished and repeated these words, and looked to see, everywhere, that mad beauty and that unspeakable value and to feel that wild joy. I don't wait anymore for egoAnn to grant me permission to notice goodness. I hold these words up before my inner eyes and challenge the gray slop of ego complaints to venture into their laser beam. The fruits of that devotion are a greatly enhanced capacity to experience and express beauty, abundance, forthrightness, and love in my daily life.

Wholeness as Harmony and Importance

Of priceless value in the report is the revelation of love as an inherent aspect of such seeing. Montague's description of "being in love with every living thing before me" stands in stark contrast to our usual human experiences of love. We begin to see that ego love is utilitarian, based upon the self's perceived needs, which it looks to the "beloved" to fill. Being focused on getting its needs met, it cannot help being self-centered and possessive. Personal love begins to be seen in its true colors in contrast with Montague's descriptions of the love-consciousness that is an unavoidable aspect of being aware of "every living thing" as a place where universal Life is living Itself, in all Its quality fullness.

> Besides all the joy and beauty and that curious sense of importance, there was a wonderful feeling of rhythm as well, only it was somehow just beyond the grasp of my mind. I heard no music, yet there was an exquisite sense of time, as though all life went by to a vast, unseen melody. Everything that moved wove out a little thread of rhythm in this tremendous whole. When a bird flew, it did so because somewhere a note had been struck for it to fly on; or else its flying struck the note; or else again the great Will that is Melody willed that it should fly. When people walked, somewhere they beat out a bit of rhythm that was in harmony with the whole great theme.

I quoted this passage in a talk that I once gave, which was taped. One man played this part of the tape every night just before going to bed. He reported that listening to that passage insured the best sleep he had ever enjoyed. I think that's because there is nothing so relaxing to the poor little separate ego as a feeling of being part of a benevolent wholeness.

Being aware only from the ego standpoint of separate materiality, we have no sense of an overall harmony and consequently no way of discovering the devastating disruption and distraction that that fragmented sense imposes on us. Having listened, so to speak, only to a radio frequency in which the program is nearly inaudible due to static, we assume the static to be "normal." Bliss reports tune us in to a pure frequency with virtually no static at all. As a result, we begin to notice and resent the "normal" static of ego living. We lose our appetite for the discordance of the ego viewpoint, yearning to hear only the pure, glad sounds of Soul.

In the paragraph above, Montague communicates something of what it feels like to actually experience that we "live and move and have our being" in God. There is no loss of individuality, either subjectively or in the details seen, yet there is a "wonderful" and "exquisite" feeling of everything being harmoniously related to Something — "Will ...Melody...the whole great theme" — in which everything finds its unity and its significance.

I have found this sense of significance or importance of particular interest and relevance. She clarifies it further in the next paragraph:

> Then, the extraordinary importance of everything! Every living creature was intensely alive and intensely beautiful, but it was as well of a marvelous value. Whether this value was in itself or a part of the whole, I could not see; but it seemed as though before my very eyes I actually beheld the truth of Christ's saying that not even a sparrow falls to the ground without the knowledge of the Father in Heaven. Yet what the importance was, I did not grasp.... But whatever it is, the importance seemed to be nearer to beauty and joy than to an anxious morality....
>
> It was perhaps as though that great value in every living thing was not so much here and now in ourselves as somewhere else. There is a great significance in every created thing, but the significance is beyond our present grasp.... All life is far more valuable than we ever dream of its being. Perhaps the following quotation from Milton may be what I was conscious of:
>
> > What if earth
> > Be but the shadow of Heaven, and things therein
> > Each to each other like, more than on earth is thought.
>
> What if here we are only symbols of ourselves, and our real being is somewhere else, — perhaps in the heart of God? Certainly that unspeakable importance had to do with our relationship to the great Whole.

Being-Value, Not Doing-Value

Struggling with language and a two-year-old memory of the experience, Montague finds it almost impossible to communicate her sense
of the "unspeakable value" of everything. Yet I think she does better than she knows. What comes across by the end of her article is
the *givenness* of things, the inherent value and importance of Life
by virtue of Its nature. This is what sets the divine standpoint apart,
absolutely, from the human. Spiritual reality is done, finished, whole.
Personal sense is always on the way to something never quite reached.
But Soul is the awareness of the already fullness of quality Life. The
dynamism of our lives lies in the expression of the inherent value and
importance of Life, not in the quest to make or find some value for
ourselves.

One of the striking features of the celebrity scene in our culture,
which was graphically revealed in the O. J. Simpson case, is that so
many people see their own lives as so valueless that they seek vicarious
importance through the most tenuous contacts with famous people.
One woman featured in a news story visited the store where Simpson
had bought a knife the week before his wife's murder. She was there,
she said, in order to "find a place in history." And a sign posted by
neighbors of the victim, sick of the harassment of sight-seers crowding
their street, read: "Get a life. Go home and live your own so we can
live ours in peace."

"Get a life...." Unfortunately, that's what the hoards of visitors are
trying to do. Looking outside of ourselves to find validation of the
importance of our lives, we are bound to come up short. Looking
outside we can only compare with other persons, and there are always those who seem to have more interesting, more important lives
than we. Then we may feel driven to pursue a sense of vicarious importance through some — any — connection to a more important
person.

Montague's report tells us that Life has Its own "unspeakable joy,
beauty, and importance." And these can only be found within, by coming home to our own Soul eyes. Soul looks for and sees and cherishes
the qualities that fill the universe, giving to all shapes and forms of life
an unspeakable value and goodness.

Loyalty to Beauty and Goodness

After a number of other illuminating comments, Montague makes the following statement:

> And all the beauty is forever there before us, forever piping to us, and we are forever failing to dance. We could not help but dance if we could see things as they really are. Then we should...fling our bodies, hearts, minds and souls into life with a glorious abandonment, an extravagant, delighted loyalty, knowing that our wildest enthusiasm cannot more than brush the hem of the real beauty and joy and wonder that is always there.

"And all the beauty is forever there before us." Time and time again, these words come to me, simultaneously breaking and healing my heart. They break my heart because they make me aware, first, of how often I fail to dance, seemingly preferring the limping lameness of egoAnn sense. But my heart is healed by hearing that, despite the ego's obscuring lens, Life's beauty is always here. These words give us the most important information possible: that the way things really are is not adequately represented by our usual ways of thinking and seeing. So we don't have to consider our ordinary personal scene the last word on life. In fact, we obviously have a life task of *not* settling for our little personal identities, but of looking to see something beyond them. Soul is always seeing and dancing to Life's beautiful music.

Seeing what really is, Montague says, gives us "an extravagant, delighted loyalty" to life, to real Life, good Life, Soul Life. Having tasted the good of our true being, the good of reality, that good becomes our highest loyalty. Even if we have so far only slight acquaintance with a spiritual, quality sense of Life, we can honor what we know of It. Being loyal to what we know of spiritual good opens the door to more and more awareness of it.

Montague's words invite us to evaluate our own operating loyalties. I know of a woman who burst into tears when a relative received a birthday card that wished her continuing "beauty, joy, grace, peace and love." The woman cried, "I've never had any of those things in my life," and she felt very sorry for herself. She was unaware that her loyalty was to a picture of herself as deprived. Her parents had divorced when she was young, and she repeatedly voiced the belief that "I will never have the family that I need." Her loyalty to that sad picture not only manifested as manic depressive emotionalism but as a pattern of manipulative and hostile behavior toward others, whom she blamed for depriving her. Her ego identity was so captivated by its story of deprivation that it never even noticed the steadfast love and support of many people in her life, the beauty that surrounded her, the grace and goodness of her experience that were evident to others.

We can discover where our loyalties lie by examining what we spend most of our time thinking about. Check your thinking out several times a day, and identify what sense of yourself and life your ego is loyal to. You may discover that ego identity is keeping you loyal to all manner of negative beliefs and the painful feelings to which they give rise. Then contrast those loyalties with Life's loyalty to Its harmony, beauty, love, intelligence, joy, and peace.

I felt at one point in my life like someone sitting in a dark theater running and rerunning old Perils of Pauline — actually, Perils of Ann — movies. I was vaguely aware that outside the sun was shining on a radiant, colorful world. I wanted to get up and walk out the door. Yet I saw myself repeatedly tugged back into a fearful fascination with the pictures playing out on the screen by the belief that I was the heroine of the drama. The ego can't help being loyal to itself. But we can discover Soul as the truth of us. Then Soul's loyalty to Its quality goodness begins to replace our compulsive attraction to ego images. Think of the transformation that would take place in every aspect of human affairs, individually and collectively, if each individual's highest loyalty were to seeing and living the qualities of spiritual good!

Montague goes on:

> And even if there is no other life, this life here and now, if we could but open our dull eyes to see it in its truth, is lovely enough to require no far-off Heaven for its justification. Heaven, in all its springtide of beauty, is here and now, before our very eyes, surging up to our very feet, lapping against our hearts. . . .

> And though I have never again touched the fullness of that ecstatic vision, I know all created things to be of a beauty and

value unspeakable, and I shall not fail to pay homage to all the loveliness with which existence overflows.

Loyalty to the good yields Montague's commitment to "pay homage to all the loveliness with which existence overflows." This statement of commitment is a pledge against the Soul betrayal that is the inevitable consequence of an ego viewpoint. The thrill and satisfaction of quality Life, once glimpsed, refine our appetites. Paying homage to the loveliness of existence, old ego allegiances begin to pale. I often ask myself: "If heaven, in all its springtide of beauty, is here and now lapping against my heart, what *am* I trying, so frantically and frustratingly, to get for myself out there?"

Montague continues:

Nor shall I fear to accord to all of life's experiences, whether sad or gay, as high, as extravagant, and as undismayed a tribute of enthusiasm as I am capable of.

Enthusiasm means "possessed by God." Soul's seeing of the divine good fills us with enthusiasm for "all of life's experiences," no matter what ego says is going on. Ego eyes will never cease to see all manner of difficulties. But what will we worship? To what pay homage? The more our loyalty is to spiritual goodness, the less impressed we will be by the claims of sin and suffering. It is not so hard to take suffering seriously. I have found it far harder to take God and goodness seriously, but that's the challenge. Montague's unflinching enthusiasm both humbles and inspires me.

CHAPTER 2

Soul Names

To him that overcometh will I give to eat of the hidden manna, and will give him a white stone, and in the stone a new name written, which no man knoweth saving he that receiveth it.
— REVELATION 2:17

My mother, Mary, lived with us for a number of years before her death at age ninety-two. She was a reticent woman who kept her problems to herself and minded her own business, so I knew very little about her sense of herself from direct communication. But I began to piece together her concerns from little vignettes that she sometimes shared with me. One day I found her fretting, and she told me that she felt troubled about something that had happened when she was a small child. She was embarrassed that it still bothered her, since it seemed so insignificant. But when I invited her to tell me the story, she did.

As a little girl, she had a cat named Whitefoot, whom she dearly loved. One day an uncle, who owned a lumber yard, came to visit. Seeing Whitefoot, he commented to my grandfather that he was having trouble with mice at the lumber yard, and he could use a good mouser. My grandfather promptly suggested that he take Whitefoot with him, which he did.

"I never saw Whitefoot again," my mother said, "except for once, when I visited the lumber yard, and I saw him wandering around, looking so lost and sad. I have never forgiven myself that I did not stand up for him and tell my uncle that he couldn't take him away from me. And it still bothers me, that I was so wishy washy, and I let him be taken away to that yard, where he was so lonely."

We talked about the incident, and I assured her that her behavior was both understandable and appropriate and that Whitefoot wasn't as sad as she presumed. I suggested that she was projecting her own sadness and sense of having betrayed him onto the cat. And she felt relieved and reassured. But later, as I thought about the continuing emotional charge of that scene to my mother, it became clear to me that it represented, not the betrayal of Whitefoot, but the betrayal of Mary. It was herself she did not stand up for, her love for and loyalty to her cat and her desire to keep him for herself. And one reason it still bothered her so much at age eighty-four was that that scene pictured forth a life-long sense of what life required of her: sacrificing her own good for the sake of others' needs and wants. This was the code of women of her class and era, and again and again throughout her life she met this requirement without questioning it. But she once said, "I don't like to think too much. If you think too much you might start to doubt and then..."

My mother, by her own account, had a very good, long life. Yet I saw her perplexed and agitated in her final, two-week illness. It seemed to me that she was trying to find a sense of resolution and completion that would allow a peaceful release of her personal story. And, to my perception, she never did. The expression on her face at the end was one of resignation and fatigue, not of resolution.

Soul Betrayal

My own sense of her code, as it was passed on to me, was that keeping others comfortable was the priority, whatever the cost to one's own peace and well-being. Such a self-sacrificing mode of living is very painful and creates an expectancy of reward that can never be fulfilled. Even so, simply becoming self-assertive instead of self-sacrificing isn't a satisfactory solution either, since others may then seem required to sacrifice their best interests to ours. In a self-and-others view of the world, there seems no other alternative.

There is no interpersonal solution to problems that reflect the inner betrayal of Soul that takes place in the misperception of ourselves as persons. We are not to blame for that misperception, but we can awaken to it and to the pattern of betrayal to which our ego identity leads us.

Psychologist Abraham Maslow discovered an "intrinsic conscience" based upon our essential human nature. He wrote:

> This [conscience] is based upon the unconscious and precon-
> scious perception of our own nature, of our own destiny, of
> our own capacities, of our own "call" in life. It insists that we
> be true to our inner nature and that we do not deny it out of
> weakness or for advantage or for any other reason. He who
> belies his talent, the born painter who sells stockings instead,
> the intelligent man who lives a stupid life, the man who sees
> the truth and keeps his mouth shut, the coward who gives up
> his manliness, all these people perceive in a deep way that they
> have done wrong to themselves and despise themselves for it.[3]

This discovery led Maslow to make a revolutionary commentary on the source and nature of evil: "What we call evil behavior appears most often to be a secondary reaction to frustration of this intrinsic nature."[4] I am increasingly convinced that not only all personal problems, but all social problems as well, have their basis in this unwitting denial of our Soulness — our intrinsic nature and conscience — which is automatic in an ego-centered perspective on life.

Believing ourselves to be separate, autonomous body/minds called persons, we seek outside of ourselves for that which will protect, nurture, and validate us. In the very turning outward, we deny the self-protective, self-nurturing, self-expressive wholeness of our being. This leads to the self-hatred to which Maslow points. Moreover, because the outward quest can never fulfill the inner longing, it is inherently frustrating, and the frustration usually gets directed outward against those to whom one has mistakenly looked for fulfillment. Blame of parents, spouses, children, friends, employers, neighbors, elected officials in local, state, and national governments — ultimately, blame of God — follows naturally from the initial mistake.

The interpersonal search for a sense of wholeness and goodness ends in disappointment and frustration, because the very premise that another person can give us, or withhold from us, permission to value ourselves is outrageous and demeaning. To stand before another human being and ask, in effect, "Please may I discover, value, affirm, enjoy, and love myself?" is clearly an irrational act. By what power or authority could another grant such an inherent right? Yet from infancy on, this pursuit of interpersonal validation governs human life.

Being "Born Again" as Soul, Not Ego

The only real alternative to problems of ego identity lies in discovering our sacred identity, Soul. The New Testament refers to the need for a new identity with various metaphors: being "born again," "putting on the new man," becoming "a new creature," and putting "new wine into new wineskins," as well as in the quote from Revelation, which promises "to him that overcometh" a "new name." The message is that our human birth identity, symbolized by our personal names, must be transcended if we are to "see the kingdom of God" and claim our spiritual potential. We cannot remain in the old constructs of thought and at the same time discover and live out from the fullness of our true being.

Those who overcome limited human identity through Soul awareness are given "to eat of the hidden manna." That's Soul food — real Soul food: the consciousness of the vast reservoirs of divine Life and Love. Jesus said, "I have meat to eat that ye know not of." Often in the past few years, I have thought of how I daily feast on spiritual ideas and qualities. I truly can affirm that "I have meat to eat that the world knows not of." This is the "hidden manna" of Soul awareness, a "table prepared in the wilderness" of material belief, which only awaits our discovery of it.

In increasing Soul awareness, we find our human name yielding to a Soul name. It is a subjective name, the inner sense of certainty that nobody else can even guess at. But we know the stuff of the new name. "Name" refers to "nature," so one's Soul name points to the spiritual, quality nature of one's true being. Finding our Soul name is an experiential process of seeing through the negative aspects associated with our human identity.

The new name comes for most of us as a slow dawning in consciousness that need not be either painful or dramatic. In fact, Soul is not dramatic at all and may therefore escape our notice unless we are paying careful attention. I became aware of the dawning of a positive, quality sense when my husband and I were in Colorado a few years ago to lead a retreat and to give workshops at a Denver church. My mother had been born and raised in Denver, the daughter of a gold miner who had hit it rich and made a substantial fortune before the vein of gold had disappeared at a fault line. Grandpa Lee had built a big house from brown stone left over from the building of the Brown Palace Hotel. Mother had talked a lot about "the old house" over the years, and I had seen it once when I was a little girl, but it had meant nothing to me.

As I thought about returning to Denver, however, the idea came to look up the old house, even though I had never had any great interest in researching my personal roots. I knew the house was being preserved as a state historical landmark, and it suddenly seemed worth a visit. But where on earth could I find the address? My mother had passed on years ago. Rummaging around in an old file drawer, I found a battered photo album and opened to a page showing sepia photos of a big house nearly buried in snow: "the great blizzard of eighteen ninety-something-or-other," I remembered. And there was the address, written below the photo in my mother's handwriting, evidence of her love for and attachment to her childhood home.

"Oh, I know where that street is," declared the friend who picked us up at the Denver airport. "We can easily swing past there on our way to the church." We drove through a transitional neighborhood and stopped before an old, slightly shabby house that is now being used as an executive office building. Entering, we found a receptionist's desk with a young woman behind it and a tall, attractive, professional-looking woman standing nearby. "May I help you?" the receptionist inquired. With a sudden rush of emotion that stung my eyes, I said, "My grandfather built this house."

"Oh," both women exclaimed, with a delight that surprised me. "You must let me show you around this wonderful old house," said the professional woman, a renter of one of the offices. She took us from bottom to top, four stories in all, and pointed out the many signs of past glory: the marble mantles and panels around the fireplaces, the huge bay windows, the hand-carved bannisters.

There was the basement, where my stern, Quaker grandfather had installed a pool table for his three obstreperous sons, and had it removed, without a word, when he discovered that the boys were playing for pennies. There was the staircase to the upstairs bedrooms, at the foot of which my grandfather would stand and shout for the children. My mother remembered hearing the drill-sergeant voice calling the boys' names: "Howard! Ralph! Naylor!" And then the sudden shift to sweetness as he called for his little girl, the apple of his eye: "Mary, dear, are you ready yet?"

I left the house in a glow of gratitude, a sense of enormous blessing. I felt that I had found out something important about my mother and, derivatively, about myself. She grew up in a mansion; she was a child of abundance and nurture! Somehow the self-denying flavor of her Quaker/Methodist upbringing and the financial struggles of the Depression years had left her of frugal mind and sternly disciplined emotion. Being very much my mother's daughter, I shared that mentality, the sense that one is here for disciplined service. Personal pleasure is suspect and tightly governed. My grandfather allowed himself one cigar a day but believed in leaving the dining table "a little bit hungry." Thus, the name Ann, like the name Mary, had meant self-sacrifice and self-discipline, a sense of burden with minimal reward.

I had also become aware, especially as I grew older, of the positive gifts of my mother's consciousness. She had an eye for beauty that saw fresh loveliness in every change of scene. A landscape that seemed dull and empty to my gaze turned into a fascinating palette of subtle shades and colors through her eyes. A soaring bird or a lone blossom evoked a gasp of appreciation from her. And sitting in our backyard after she came to live with us in her eighties, she declared it to be "paradise park."

Yet for me it was the austere, self-sacrificing sense that had formed the foundation of my own human identity. And now the visit to "the old house" began to dissolve the ego blinders. Throughout the weekend, signs of spiritual nurture continued to appear. On the final day, my husband, Jan, and I were sitting in a church pew, waiting to announce our afternoon workshops. I was feeling completely drained by the demands of retreat leadership and was wondering how I could make it through an afternoon workshop with an entirely new group of people. Then the lights in the sanctuary dimmed, and a man with a beautiful baritone voice began singing a song I had never heard before. It ended with this verse:

> I've dreamed of Eden all my life,
> I find it more and more each day.

Now everywhere I go across the land,
I stand so proudly in the sun and say,
"I am home."[5]

My mother's favorite brother had had a glorious baritone voice. She had often told me of what a delight his singing had been to her on many occasions. The special serendipity of this singer and this song, which so resonated with my sense of homecoming, made it a moment of pure grace. (We later learned that the usual soloist at this church was a woman. The baritone was a substitute for this particular day.) In just such sweet and simple ways did divine Love intrude upon and push out my negative, personal "take" on things throughout the entire weekend.

As we flew back to California, it occurred to me that I had found something more important than my human, personal roots. This experience had put me in touch with what I would now call my Soul roots. And in the months following that trip, those roots bore continued fruit as the flowering in consciousness of a sense of quality goodness underlying and surrounding me.

Finding and Following Our Bliss

In his oft-repeated injunction to "follow your bliss," Joseph Campbell addressed a great need and longing of our time. He gave us permission to honor our inner integrity, to find our Soulness and follow It rather than the "shoulds" and "have to's" of our human story names. In describing his own discovery of this principle, he wrote:

> Now, I came to this idea of bliss because in Sanskrit, which is the great spiritual language of the world, there are three terms that represent the brink, the jumping-off place to the ocean of transcendence: *Sat, Chit, Ananda*. The word *"Sat"* means being. *"Chit"* means consciousness. *"Ananda"* means bliss or rapture. I thought, "I don't know whether my consciousness is proper consciousness or not; I don't know whether what I know of my being is my proper being or not; but I do know where my rapture is. So let me hang on to rapture, and that will bring me both my consciousness and my being." I think it worked. . . .

Each person can have his own depth experience and some conviction of being in touch with his own *sat-chit-ananda*, his own being through consciousness and bliss.[6]

The injunction to "follow your bliss" points us precisely to our Soul identity, which is our being as the consciousness of bliss. That identity then yields the life agenda of letting *that* name-being-consciousness-bliss express and fulfill Itself as quality living in the highest appreciable forms for each individual.

Soul is that conscious awareness, the "secret place of the most High" within which and from which we experience our own lives as increasingly expressive, creative, healthy, beautiful, good, pure, innocent, joyful, and effortless. Those qualities are the substance of divine Life, and they take shape as the highest forms of good that an individual can allow.

For example, for a person whose identity sense is that of a homeless derelict, a hot meal at a mission may be the highest appreciable form of supply and nurture. For Malcolm Forbes, whose identity sense was of a billionaire business magnate, a birthday party in Morocco, with four hundred guests from around the world, expressed his highest appreciable sense of those same divine qualities.

The spiritual facts of supply and nurture are the same, and Soul knows them in their completeness. But the capacity of the individual to experience and express these Soul realities will vary greatly according to the degree of obfuscation in the human identity lens. If the homeless individual can recognize the goodness of the hot meal and the mission cot as evidences of a larger goodness, then the lens of deprivation will begin to melt. More evidence of quality Life will be allowed to shine through, and the identity of lack will begin to yield.

Judging "with Right Judgment"

If we want to experience more spiritual good than we are currently capable of, we can stretch our capacity for the good by learning to "judge with right judgment" (John 7:24, RSV). Moments of Soul awareness seem sporadic and occasional because the ego leads us to pay attention to surface, material, and interpersonal details, to "judge by appearances." Attention is captured by the foreground, the separate-thingness of human experience, and the background, which is nondimensional and universal, goes largely unnoticed.

For example, while driving the freeways of Southern California I am sometimes embarrassed to notice how much of the time I am mentally, and sometimes verbally, muttering about the ineptitude or inconsideration of other drivers. Yet occasionally I will notice the incredible miracle of it all: that all these seemingly separate mind/bodies, each ensconced in its metal container, whizzing along at seventy miles an hour, still manage, mostly, to reach their destinations unscathed. And I am then aware that we all "live and drive and have our being" in that universal energy Field of Love/Intelligence that is God.

I once shared a story I had heard with one of my sons. It was about a woman who was showing her spiritual teacher around her backyard. The teacher commented on the number of birds. The woman exclaimed, "Oh, I never noticed any birds out here before." Her teacher replied, "Madam, you must have birds in your heart before you will find birds in your backyard."

Some weeks later, I came fresh and fuming off the freeway and regaled my son with an account of "some jerk" who had nearly caused an accident. He brought me up short with the comment, "Madam, you must have jerks in your heart before you will find jerks on the freeway." I guess it follows as well that we must have harmony and order in our hearts before we will notice them on the freeway.

In a culture in which simple traffic altercations can turn into murderous assaults, driving "in Soul" rather than "in ego" is not just an exercise in aesthetics. The Soul awareness of the laws of harmony and good can save our lives. It can actually operate to neutralize the toxic mentalities around us. Learning to Soul-see throughout the day, whether we are driving or watching TV, is the only way to be assured of some degree of safety, health, and quality living.

In my case, increasing Soul awareness is leading to a greater sense of being an artist of Life rather than a problem-solver or ignorance-corrector. Where egoAnn had represented a sense of self-sacrifice, effort, burden, and lack, SoulAnn's name, or nature, is emerging as grace, effortlessness, support, and abundance. The sense of being valuable as a meeter-of-needs is being replaced by a cherishing of the inherent value of Life. This is unfolding as fresh ideas about artistic forms of writing and a possible move to a different location. Perhaps most importantly, it is dissolving the sense that everything that needs to be done around the house and the yard is a chore. That sense had hung like a drab, cold curtain in my consciousness for as long as I can remember.

The surprise of Soul identity is that the more we look to see and cherish and celebrate *universal* qualities, the more the *specific* details of our individual lives unfold in the most satisfying and fulfilling ways. In finding and honoring our Soul identity, we can be certain of the fulfillment of our very best "human" potential.

Soul Teachers and Mentors

We all have had people in our experience who have encouraged the best in us. When we are young, teachers, ministers, or coaches often play such a role. As adults, we may consciously seek out mentors. In college and seminary, I found certain faculty members becoming, spontaneously, nurturing friends and guides. For more concentrated help, I sought out a psychotherapist, and when psychological work was finished, a spiritual teacher came naturally into my experience. When I had learned all I could from him, another teacher, who lifted my thought still higher, appeared.

Sometimes our teachers are living individuals; sometimes a specific book or formulation by someone we have never met guides our way. While in New York during my college years, I wandered into the Madison Avenue Presbyterian Church, where the preaching of Dr. George Buttrick lifted me out of a desert of doubt and confusion. Later, while training as a psychotherapist, my required "training analysis" turned into years of spiritual growth under the guidance of Dr. Thomas Hora, whose inspired thinking became identified as Metapsychiatry. During my years with Dr. Hora, the writings of Joel Goldsmith, Mary Baker Eddy, and various Zen Buddhist teachers also nurtured my spiritual understanding. Never have I been without fresh, inspiring spiritual mentors, in print or in person. Since Soul is already the truth of our being, it must and does continue to appear in the form of appropriate teachers and mentors at every stage, if we are interested in understanding more.

In addition to the obviously "spiritual" guides, I have been delighted to find that Soul awareness brings a receptivity to spiritual nurture in the most surprising places. Mary Baker Eddy writes, "As mortals gain more correct views of God and man, multitudinous objects of creation, which before were invisible, will become visible."[7]

This has certainly proved true for me. In the past several years, I have found great Soul riches in such diverse locations as Ellis Peters's murder mystery series entitled *The Chronicles of Brother Cadfael* and movies such as *Enchanted April* and *Forrest Gump*. The popularity of these books and films attests to the increasing capacity in our culture to appreciate spiritual values.

When we look around the world through ego eyes, everything and everybody else seems to be outside of us and therefore separate from us. When we see beautiful sights or beautiful things, when we notice positive behavior in others or see people who seem to possess capabilities we'd like to have, these observations serve to underscore our feeling of separation from the good. Jealousy and envy are the inevitable offspring of this sense of separation. When others seem to have goods of which we seem to be deprived, personhood is driven to try to get that good for itself through possession or rivalry. Failing that, malice rears its ugly head in the desire to spoil the good of the other that seems to elude us. Ego can't help these feelings. But we can observe them, realize their spoiler-source, and let the excruciating pain of envy and malice drive us to Soul's viewpoint.

Soul eyes give us a different take on what seems to be going on outside of ourselves. Having discovered that the seeing of beauty *is* beauty seeing itself, we can consciously identify with every quality perceived. The trick is in understanding that the quality is the real good of anything. So in seeing the quality, we discover that it already "belongs" to us. Consciously celebrating the quality we see as the truth of our own lives is a way of practicing our Soul names.

For example, where I used to be envious of larger, more beautiful homes in our neighborhood, I now enjoy the sense of wealth and beauty of which they make me aware. A mansion to fund and care for isn't *my* cup of tea; I don't want the bother of the upkeep. But I am glad that richness and beauty are expressed in such ways. I get to enjoy looking at them without the hassle of owning them.

Quality-seeing takes away the pain of located, limited goodness.

When our older son, Tom, was a baby, I was wheeling him in his carriage on a New York street. We stopped to wait for a traffic light to change. An elderly woman standing next to me suddenly blurted out, "It's a terrible thing for such a beautiful baby to be born into such an ugly world!"

I was shocked by her outburst and did not know what to reply. But later I wished I had been able to say to her, "But you see, if such a beautiful baby can be born, it cannot be such an ugly world." Any beauty says, "Life is beautiful," and if Life is beautiful, then *my* life is beautiful. I only need to learn to claim my seeing as the truth of my being.

Soul Journaling

Many people practice keeping a journal of their thoughts and insights. This can be a very enriching practice. Once we distinguish between our human sense and Soul's sense of things, we can add a variation to journaling that enables us to be, so to speak, our own counselors and practitioners, or better, to let Soul guide and heal us.

When you feel really disturbed, it is useful to follow this procedure:

1. Identify the feelings that are disturbing you. "Feeling upset" is not specific enough. Do you feel sadness, fear, anger, hurt, resentment? Write it down. Then ask yourself, "What belief feels this way?"

2. Write down the beliefs that underlie and give rise to the feelings and confusion. If you aren't sure how to identify a belief, ask, "If I gave this feeling words, what would it say?" Then write down, as specifically as possible, the thoughts behind the feelings.

For example, perhaps the thought is something like, "I feel hurt because my boss didn't recognize my work today," or "I'm angry because my wife didn't want sex last night, and it makes me feel unloved." This surface belief is only an excuse for the feeling. Underneath that is a basic identity belief about ourselves.

3. Take the belief to a deeper level. See how this seeming interpersonal glitch and your feelings about it reflect a sense of how things always go for you. Underneath chronic negative feelings there is a belief that "I *always*..." or "I *never*...." get this or that. When you get to that "always" belief, you have identified a pillar of your ego identity.

Write it down: "Nobody ever appreciates me!" "I never get the love I need." Then look at it as *just a belief.* Ask yourself if you like that belief and want it to live through you. If not, then acknowledge your Soul identity and declare Its seeing.

4. Seek the spiritual counterfact by reversing the ego claim. Since problems are pointers, we let the negative beliefs point us to the positive, spiritual truth of being. Spirit is universal, and Its qualities are everywhere, all the time. There cannot actually be a lack of love, appreciation, or any other aspect of the good. Problems are always a consequence of a constricted, located belief obscuring our awareness of what is fully present at that moment.

So we ask what the belief of being deprived or hurt points us to, by reversal, and it is universal Love. Clearly, if we were aware of universal Love, we would not feel deprived or hurt. Likewise, the beliefs of effort and stress point us to grace. Need and lack point us to abundance and completeness. Write down these Soul qualities. Each ego problem informs us of the specific aspect of spiritual good that we are being robbed of seeing, at this moment. So the solution lies in letting Soul show us what *It* is seeing right here, right now.

Having identified the spiritual facts, we can consciously look to see evidences of those realities in our experience. We can call to mind the many times when, despite the ego's insistence, Life has manifested Its goodness in appreciable forms. Paying attention to what really is, we are gradually lifted above the belief, hence the feeling, of limited personal life and mind. Claiming Soul qualities as already ours, we begin to "have" — and thus be in a position to receive more of — the good that material belief declares we "have not." Soul journaling is thus a way to invite Soul awareness to address, directly, the problems to which our ego names give rise.

Soul Seeing Reports

I know of no more enlightening description of the shift from ego identity to Soul identity than the following report. It is by a woman who had been previously healed of physical and mental suffering through reading *Science and Health* by Mary Baker Eddy. She writes:

For a long time I was always looking back to see if the error had gone, until one day when I realized that to catch a glimpse of what spiritual sense means I must put corporeal sense behind me. I then set to work in earnest to find the true way. I opened Science & Health and these words were before me, "If God were understood, instead of being merely believed, this understanding would establish health" (p. 203). I saw that I must get the right understanding of God!

I closed the book and with head bowed in prayer I waited with longing intensity for some answer. How long I waited I do not know, but suddenly, like a wonderful burst of sunlight after a storm, came clearly this thought, "Be still, and know that I am God." I held my breath — deep into my hungering thought sank the infinite meaning of that "I." All self-conceit, egotism, selfishness, everything that constitutes the mortal "I" sank abashed out of sight. I trod, as it were, on holy ground. Words are inadequate to convey the fullness of that spiritual uplifting, but others who have had similar experiences will understand.

From that hour I have had an intelligent consciousness of the ever-presence of an infinite God who is only good.[8]

There is a sense of radical release in this woman's description of ego identity sinking "abashed out of sight." Seen from the standpoint of the staggering grandeur of universal Life, human self sense looks ludicrous. It simply self-destructs, leaving the field of awareness to Soul's "intelligent consciousness of" the divine Presence.

One of the "Illuminating Letters" written in response to the publication of "Twenty Minutes of Reality" describes the following realization, which gives us another form of Soul realization:

Several "Twenty Minutes of Reality" have come to me later in life. Once at a great crisis, a mental strain, accompanied with a humiliating sense of inability to act strongly, I had a sudden vision of a central self which almost overwhelmed me. It was a reservoir of new, unguessed powers, measureless capacities, and unfathomed emotions — a reservoir from which I had never drawn because this present life offered neither time nor scope for what was there, and I involuntarily exclaimed, "Now I *know* I am immortal! I am more than I dreamed I was."

The painful experience of the restriction and inadequacy of ego led in this case to the momentary release of that limiting sense and the revelation of Soul identity. The writer explains the previous unawareness of this grand identity in external terms — "this present life offered neither time nor scope for what was there" — but that is the effect, not the cause of the narrowness of viewpoint. This discovery led the writer to an awareness of immortality, but seemingly not to a realization that much more of that spiritual identity/reservoir could be manifested in "this life." The writer shares other glimpses and then adds: "I feel that I ought to apologize because, having found one to understand, I have spoken. Yet, why should not spies who have seen the Promised Land compare their bunches of grapes on their return?"[9]

Even more, why should not those who have seen the Promised Land share their visions with those who have yet to see it, or even those who are unaware that there is such a thing? God knows, the ego world is committed enough to sharing — and insisting upon — its nightmares of horror and ugliness. I like to think of all those who have traversed unusual heights of consciousness as "spiritual astronauts" whose reports are even more important to humankind and the planet than are those of the space explorers of our time.

One of the first bliss reports that became a major Soul map for me was the testimony of the "Canadian housewife" in the book *The Three Pillars of Zen*, by Roshi Philip Kapleau. Years after her initial breakthrough, the writer experienced a spontaneous ego loss of great magnitude. She wrote:

> The next morning, just after breakfast, I suddenly felt as though I were being struck by a bolt of lightning, and I began to tremble. All at once the whole trauma of my difficult birth flashed into my mind. Like a key, this opened dark rooms of secret resentments and hidden fears, which flowed out of me like poisons. Tears gushed out and so weakened me I had to lie down. Yet a deep happiness was there.... Slowly my focus changed: "I'*m* dead! There's nothing to call *me*! There never was a *me*! It's an allegory, a mental image, a pattern upon which nothing was ever modeled." I grew dizzy with delight.

Solid objects appeared as shadows, and everything my eyes fell upon was radiantly beautiful.

This was the first report I had ever encountered of the realization that "There's nothing to call *me!* It's an allegory, a mental image, a pattern upon which nothing was ever modeled." That this discovery should then lead to being "dizzy with delight" and seeing everything as "radiantly beautiful" was greatly enlightening and something that I pondered for many months. Among the writer's further revelations are the following:

> The least expression of weather variation, a soft rain or a gentle breeze, touches me as a — what can I say? — miracle of unmatched wonder, beauty, and goodness. There is nothing to do: just to be is a supremely total act. . . .
>
> I feel a love which, without object, is best called lovingness. But my old emotional reactions still coarsely interfere with the expressions of this supremely gentle and effortless lovingness. . . .
>
> I feel a consciousness which is neither myself nor not myself, which is protecting or leading me into directions helpful to my proper growth and maturity, and propelling me away from that which is against that growth. It is like a stream into which I have flowed and, joyously, is carrying me beyond myself.[10]

The description of a "consciousness which is neither myself nor not myself which is protecting or leading me in directions proper to my growth and maturity, and which is propelling me away from that which is against that growth" captures with great clarity the feeling and action of Soul. The growth propulsion and protection described are exact functions of our sacred identity, and they are always in operation. We are at all times being protected and led in life-enhancing directions and propelled away from destructive self-concerns. So we don't need to add anything from outside of ourselves. This "hidden manna" of guidance and protection is already within. We simply need to learn how to abandon consciousness to this Soul stream that joyously carries us beyond our *selves.*

CHAPTER 3

Soul and the Shadow

Subtle is the Lord, but malicious He is not.
— ALBERT EINSTEIN

The natural man does not receive the gifts of the Spirit of God, for they are folly to him, and he is not able to understand them because they are spiritually discerned.
— PAUL (1 CORINTHIANS 2:14, RSV)

The weekend conference unfolded beautifully. The theme was "The Balance of the Masculine and the Feminine." For a day and a half, the participants — male and female, couples and individuals — explored the fullness of spiritual identity. In the final meeting, as each shared his or her insights from the weekend, the atmosphere was as clear and radiant as the winter sunlight that flooded through the windows.

The serenity was shattered as one male participant began to speak in anguished tones. He launched into a description of his sexual torments. He graphically described the lust that sometimes overcame him and the rage-filled masturbatory practices that followed. This sudden explosion of anger shocked the group, but we all sat silently until the tirade ended.

In the hush that followed, I invited other participants to respond. Nearly all did, and in turn each spoke lovingly to him, offering encouragement and clarification. In the end, the speaker felt relieved. He could even begin to see that the beliefs that tormented him *were* beliefs, not his true identity.

Spiritual students are often surprised by the problems that arise like sudden, dark clouds in the context of the greatest spiritual light. Over the years, my husband and I have noticed that the immediate fruits of workshops for some students may be physical or emotional upsets. Many couples report that they had the worst fights of their marriages during the course of a weekend retreat.

In order to understand the phenomenon, we need to distinguish between Soul identity and ego identity. The workshop had focused exclusively on Soul identity, within which we can find our original completeness and purity. To ego, romantic love and sexual practices represent a sense of incompleteness trying to complete and fulfill itself. To Soul, they express the already established completeness of being. For some participants, the discovery of the Soul viewpoint flooded consciousness with light. It gave them a totally different sense of what love relationships were about.

For the above-mentioned man, however, the light was unbearable. His personal beliefs about himself as a man, about women, love, sex, and marriage, were so troubled and opaque that, instead of yielding to the light, they were exposed and heightened by it. The very purity and beauty of the Soul realities made his personal thoughts and feelings seem ugly and unacceptable to him. Yet he felt totally unable to see beyond them. The rage that was verbalized toward women and emotionally projected at the group failed to hide his blatant self-loathing. It seemed to him that other group members were able to find and enjoy the health and freedom of Soul while he felt trapped in his dark ego prison.

The Dynamics of Light

In physics, light dissolves darkness. In consciousness, light likewise dissolves darkness. But the more substantially we are identified with the darkness, the more likely it is that the "dark" identity sense will fight for itself before yielding. The more an ego belief feels directly addressed, the more strongly it may assert itself.

Metaphysical thinking has been prone to defining such seemingly negative ego eruptions as an intentional assault by "mortal mind" or "the anti-Christ" upon Truth. Such a definition only gives power and intelligence to something that is a mechanical, mindless operation. Although I *felt* as if some anti-Soul force were seeking to sabotage the positive fruitfulness of the weekend, I don't think that's the most helpful way to understand what took place. It is more useful to see that false beliefs are exposed by the light and will seem heightened until they are seen through. We even have a common aphorism pointing to this phenomenon: "It's always darkest before dawn."

The power is with the light because light is really all there is. Darkness is not a substance in itself. We have flash*lights* but not flash*darks*. The more our sense of substance is light, that is, the more the positive qualities of Soul seem real to us, the less impressed we are with the histrionics of personal sense.

Soul Subtlety

Einstein's statement "Subtle is the Lord, but malicious He is not" distinguishes the *seeing* issue from the *being* issue. When asked to elaborate on that statement, he replied, "Nature hides her secret because of her essential loftiness, but not by means of ruse."[11] The subtlety and loftiness of spiritual, quality Life hide It from the eyes of "the natural man," whose perspective is one "of the flesh." But the nature of "the Lord" is neither malicious nor deceptive.

From a fleshly viewpoint, life may seem to be malicious and betraying and the good, consequently, "too good to be true." The lens through which "the natural man" looks screens out the things of the Spirit, leading him to consider them "folly." To that sense of things, the spiritual viewpoint and its view may even be enraging. It seems to offer hope of something wonderful, something the little ego desperately wants to "have." Yet everything in the ego lens denies even the possibility of the goods of Spirit because it is blind to the level of consciousness upon which quality good can be discerned.

The Spoiler and the Shadow

There's no doubt that coming to terms with evil, especially our own misery and meanness, is one of the tougher issues of life. But it does help to start with a distinction between the human misconception of self/life and Soul awareness. I call the ego perspective and its feelings "the spoiler" because that's how it operates in our thinking. Since it can't be aware of universal, nondual good, it says "Yes, but ..." to every positive thing in our experience. "Yes, I know things are okay now, but it won't last." "Yes, I know you did well yesterday, but can you keep it up?" "Yes, I know that your baby is healthy now, but the flu/chicken pox/cancer is going around." The "shadow" or dark side of life, individually and collectively, is the inevitable and even necessary consequence of the ego viewpoint on life. The belief of life apart from God, of mind located in a material body, is mistaken, and therefore it is inherently troublesome. The separateness and locatedness of its viewpoint argue fear and limitation at every point. The voice of the spoiler is heard throughout the land of personal identity. It just plain feels bad to be a person, any person.

The Spell of Our Human Names

Duality — good and bad — is inherent in the seeming situation of located mind and life. Our human names identify particular characters in particular dramas. Our human lives are essentially stories, dramatic plots unfolding along a time line. Did you ever stop and think about the predicament that human identity seems to put us all in? We find ourselves in the midst of a story, having somehow been assigned to play a certain character, and the whole script seems to have been written by somebody else. We may try to take charge of the story as we get older. Indeed, in young adulthood, taking charge and making our stories go where we want them to seems like what we are required to do. But as we get older, we discover how fixed we seem to be in a script not of our own making.

In the book *A High Wind in Jamaica*, the author captures with particular poignancy the plight of personal identity as seen through the eyes of Emily, a ten-year-old girl who suddenly discovered "that she was *she*." Her first reaction came from some observation point beyond that self-identity:

> She began to laugh, rather mockingly. "Well!" she thought, in effect. "Fancy *you*, of all people, going and getting caught like this! — You can't get out of it now, not for a very long time:

you'll have to go through with being a child, and growing up, and getting old, before you'll be quit of this mad prank."

I first read this book when I was in college, and I was enormously impressed by the author's recognition of the peculiarity of this basic human situation, which goes almost totally unnoticed. Human identity a "mad prank"? Our selfhood some sort of existential joke? That's how it begins to look, as the author goes on to describe the girl's realization of being "this particular one, this Emily; born in such-and-such a year...and encased in this particular rather pleasing little casket of flesh." Emily begins to ponder the implications of her incarnation:

> Well then, granted she was Emily, what were the consequences besides enclosure in that particular little body...and lodgement behind a particular pair of eyes?
>
> It implied a whole series of circumstances. In the first place, there was her family, a number of brothers and sisters from whom, before, she had never entirely dissociated herself; but now she got such a sudden feeling of being a discrete person that they seemed as separate from her as the ship itself. However, willy-nilly, she was almost as tied to them as she was to her body....
>
> What was going to happen? Were there disasters running about loose, disasters which her rash marriage to the body of Emily Thornton made her vulnerable to?[12]

Most of us never go through the conscious recognition that being a person means being "encased in [a] particular...casket of flesh" and thereby "married" to a particular identity that ties us to other particular identities and, potentially, to whatever "disasters running about loose" those identities are "vulnerable to." But story-identity does just that. It assigns us a character identity that must live out the details of its drama. And those details will be both good and bad, just as all the characters in the story are made up of both good and bad characteristics. *Human belief-identity includes belief-shadows.*

The Dream and the Dreamer

In order to distinguish belief-experience from spiritual Life, the belief state of consciousness is often designated a "dream." This metaphor helps us understand how ego identity can feel, to itself, completely real, and yet upon "waking" be discovered to be "unreal." Personal existence seems real within its own belief universe, yet from a Soul viewpoint the only real things about it are the qualities. These spiritual qualities shine through despite, and not because of, the details of the story. The Montague report illustrates such quality discernment.

Within the dream of personal reality, shared beliefs potentiate each other. The collective shadow may assume a power and reality that wreak havoc on the cast of players. But the destruction takes place only on the level of the beliefs, only within the dream and only to the dream characters. *The essential question, then, is not "Why is this bad thing happening to me?" but "To what identity is this bad thing happening?"* The entry point to deliverance from the evil experience is as close as asking, "What is my real identity?" The universe of qualities is never touched by the cataclysms of the material scene, and this truth is of profound practicality in our human experience. (The report of Major Haswell at the end of this chapter provides stunning evidence that this is the case.)

When we come at the issue of identity from the standpoint of consciousness, we find our sense of identity reframed. Personal identity is seen to be dream identity, meaning that it is made up of mental images that exert a mesmerizing influence in consciousness. A personal name accepted as identity constitutes a spell that hypnotizes the individual into preoccupation with the details of *its* particular drama and allows little attention to anything else. The belief that mind is located within the parameters of the personal story keeps awareness confined to and preoccupied with those limits.

Self-confirmatory Thinking

Inherent to personal identity, or ego, is the drive to keep itself intact. The sense of having a particular, separate identity gives rise to a mental mechanism of self-perpetuation. This is what makes it a spell with such a hypnotizing effect. Thomas Hora terms this inherent mental drive toward the perpetuation of the beliefs with which we are identified "self-confirmatory thinking." The specific contents of the perceived self are not a factor. It makes no difference whether they are good or bad. The mechanism of self-confirmation operates to keep the entire self-identity package intact.

Nobody, consciously, wants to suffer, feel bad, experience lack, etc. Yet all of these negative feelings and conditions may belong to, and thus confirm, one's personal identity. If I see myself as inadequate, I will feel anxious and defensive. That belief and its feelings will tend to screen out evidences of adequacy, while picking up every possible evidence of inadequacy. The fact that that is a very unpleasant belief will not keep it from operating to confirm itself as true. Understanding this mechanical drive of self-sense to keep its sense of "I" intact keeps us from being either naive or judgmental toward ourselves and others. The self cannot do other than confirm itself, so there's no point in blaming it. This does not mean being passive or accepting hostile or harmful behavior. But it does mean seeing what is happening as a nonpersonal mental dynamism at work.

But what's a poor self to do if it can't help confirming itself? Deliverance, we have said, lies in asking to be shown our true identity. We want to come home to our own Soul identity, within which we automatically see the Soul identity of others. This aligns us with the best in ourselves and others rather than putting us in a position of adversarialness. And it makes clear that *identity is the issue in the experience of evil, not "evil" itself.* Hora says, "When we are tempted to engage in self-confirmatory ideation, we must quickly turn to God-confirmatory ideation. If we do this, we can always expect some favorable resolution of whatever problem we may be facing."[13]

Understanding, Not Repression

A shift in consciousness is not the same thing as repression or suppression of feelings. A failure to understand the difference creates a lot of miscommunication on the subject. Perhaps more importantly, it can lead to mentally unhealthy practices.

On one side, people who try to *believe* rather than *understand* spiritual statements end up trying to make their egos behave according to Soul standards. Ego thoughts and feelings are simply denied rather than being unmasked and seen through. Being judged unacceptable to the ego itself, such mental and emotional stuff must be stashed away somewhere, out of sight. It then is expressed symbolically, through physical and situational symptoms, or is acted out irrationally.

One man who attended a workshop of mine confided to me before the meeting that his middle-aged son lived with him and was unable to work due to mental illness. The son would suddenly explode with rage, gesticulating wildly, screaming and cursing. Afterward, if his father referred to it, he would say, "I was singing, Dad."

During the workshop, this man's contributions tended to be rather rigid statements of "truth." When someone in the group didn't immediately understand what he was saying, he would simply repeat the statement in a louder voice. He seemed fearful of letting people talk about their personal thoughts and feelings. This made him completely incapable of rewording and discussing in a relevant way the concepts that he hurled into the group's midst. It didn't take a Ph.D. in psychology to see why his son couldn't recognize and deal with his anger.

On the flip side, there are those who think we must honor every feeling that comes up. This is based on the belief that the ego's emotional effluents make up our true identity. Authenticity then requires that we allow these feelings to dictate our moods and actions. It is recognized that we've got to exercise some control over our more destructive impulses. But that's not easy when they are owned as belonging to our true identity. So people are taught to hit pillows or work out in the gym to relieve the stress of controlling their feelings.

Both of these approaches are ego-dominated. They stay on the material, personal level of thought. They are unaware of Soul and of the possibility of actually perceiving and reasoning from the level of Soul awareness. What is really useful — and it doesn't happen in a day! — is getting the right idea about who we are so that we can sort out the claims from within. The concept of Soul identity as distinct from ego identity is a tool that helps us begin to take charge of our thoughts and feelings. Feelings are clues to thoughts. Thoughts are clues to beliefs. And troublesome beliefs can be addressed and actually dissolved by *understanding* the truth of spiritual Life. This will be further discussed in the chapter on Soul-lutions. But I want to make clear at this point, that I'm not talking some Pollyanna path of repression.

Nonlocal Mind

Larry Dossey, in his enlightening book *Recovering the Soul*, describes the importance of a nonlocal concept of mind. Dr. Dossey writes:

> Something vital has been left out of almost all the modern efforts to understand our mental life — something that counts as a first principle, without which everything is bound to be incomplete and off base.
>
> This missing element is the mind's *nonlocal* nature....
>
> *Recovering the nonlocal nature of the mind ... is essentially a recovery of the soul....*
>
> Although Mind is neither confined to the brain nor a product of it, Mind may nonetheless work through the brain. The result is the appearance of individual minds, derivative of the larger Mind, which we refer to as the individual self, the ego, the person, and the sense of I.[14]

In this passage, Dossey distinguishes between the reality of nonlocal Mind and the *appearance* of individual minds and selves, the personal sense of "I." This distinction enables us to notice the fact that *experiences of evil occur within, and only within, the separate-ego beliefs about life*. Bliss testimonies reveal no such duality or negativity from the universal standpoint.

Universal Mind Is Not Collective

Indeed, bliss reports help us see clearly that on the ultimate level of perception Life is pure, spiritual substance, nondual good. One of the greatest sources of confusion in discussions about consciousness and reality is the failure to make a distinction between the absolute, divine Mind/Life, and a collective idea of consciousness, like the "force" in Star Wars terminology. Because the human lens includes opposites, dualism, and multiplicity, the idea of nondual reality is incomprehensible to it. It can only conceive of the wholeness of being as including all the dualism and multiplicity so evident on the human level. But pure Spirit, although infinitely varied, reveals Itself to be wholly good on the ultimate level. The perception of a wholeness that includes good and bad belongs to a different level of awareness.

Only when this distinction is clear can we understand that the painful and sometimes frightening surfacing of ego beliefs in the light of divine reality does not, really, touch or interact with Soul awareness. The whole disturbance takes place to and within the premise of separate, material life.

Evil Based upon Soul Betrayal

From the divine viewpoint of Soul we can see that the most horrific pictures of evil never touch real Life, which is universal and nondimensional. If we understand this, we can make sense of our experience and at the same time dethrone evil as a power. We must be able to look straight at pictures of evil, see and acknowledge the intolerable ugliness of it — as is done in a film such as *Schindler's List* — and yet we must also find a way of understanding it that punctures its pretensions and opens the door to healing and transformation.

As we saw in chapter 2, psychologist Abraham Maslow identified "evil behavior" as "a secondary reaction to the frustration of [man's] intrinsic nature." This is a denial of the conventional, Christian view that human beings are inherently sinful. *What is inherently sinful is the misconception of the human being as person.* Every one of us, because of our ego beliefs, feels alienated from the fullness of our potential. Our story identity, as we have seen, not only gives us a character to play but determines what happens to that character. Some of us seem to be born into families that give us, to some degree, the love and support that we need. Others are condemned to play characters who are abused or deprived from birth. Though the latter may blame others for their condition, the real culprit is personal identity.

It's all too arbitrary and random to be borne. And even the best human family can't give any of us the sense of wholeness for which we yearn. Every person, however positive the story, feels, by definition, separate from the good and impeded in realizing his or her highest aspirations. The sense of being cut off, by virtue of who we think we are, from our own completeness is intolerable.

I recently saw an interview on TV with a savage gang killer, who will be released onto the streets in a few years. He has totally intellectualized his murders, declaring them part of a war and therefore as legitimate as any wartime killings of the enemy. But when asked about his feelings for his natural father, a professional football player who had neglected him, he first voiced his rage: "I hate him." Then, astonishingly, tears came to his eyes as he continued, "Because of what I could have been if he had been a real father to me." Clearly, it was the sense of the loss of his own capacities and possibilities that was so painful to him.

Reports of the torture of children reveal the mental pictures that claim to be the identity of the abuser. These pictures reveal individuals who feel so alienated from their own innocence and purity that they must either try to damage those qualities in others or try by the grossest of means to appropriate them from another. The cannibal murderer of the 1980s Jeffrey Dahmer made a statement to the effect that if he could have had some sort of normal affection and love relationships, he would not have felt compelled to commit his monstrous acts. In primitive, cannibal societies, eating captured enemies is the way to appropriate their qualities. It's an unspeakably vile picture to our level of thought. But it is better to understand the meaning of it than to yield to the fearful revulsion that seeks the solution in simply killing the "monster."

Given the nature of self-confirmatory thinking, we must not be so naive as to think that such primitive and hideously distorted ego sense will easily yield to spiritual identity. Indeed, within the context of human thinking and culture, individuals identified with beliefs that threaten the well-being of others need to be kept out of circulation for the good of all. But understanding that people are not intentionally evil could provide the basis for a more enlightened penal system than that based upon the belief that punishment is a deterrent. We presumably want those who are going to be released back onto the streets to be changed for the good. A change for the good requires intensive exposure to quality goodness, education, and help in understanding and releasing the beliefs that make up that ego identity.

Many reporters of bliss experiences comment at the end that that one glimpse of the universe of Soul has given them a stability and an equanimity through times of personal crisis that they would never have had otherwise. Having once plumbed the depths of the ocean of divine Life and Love, they could ride out the waves of personal experience with a greater confidence. The less impressed we are with the details of our human stories, the less disturbed we are by them.

As I sat with my mother during her final years and heard again and again the stories of her childhood, I began to get a sense of the ephemeral nature of human experience, which has been very useful to me. She loved to ramble on about events in her early years, the good times with family and friends. It occurred to me that she was the only one left in whose memory bank these things still lived on. Once she was gone, I realized, there would be nobody who remembered them. These events would have disappeared from the face of the earth. And, I thought, if such experiences end up being nothing at all, how real can they have ever been? Yes, the ego's experiences are real and important to itself at the time. But clearly they have no ultimate reality.

This observation has helped me be less impressed with egoAnn's tale of woe. I can feel as bad as the next person, but I don't *believe* those feelings so much anymore. So the bad feelings don't last as long and aren't as intense as before. Sometimes, identifying the sad, sad story underneath the feeling, I ask myself, "Does the universe know about this? Has this impacted divine Life in some way?" If not, then perhaps I don't need to spend such a great deal of time wallowing in, managing, or trying to escape the muck.

Soul's Initiative

However furiously the ego may protest being exposed and dissolved by the light of Soul, the entire process is at the initiative of Soul, not of ego or of evil. The voice of Soul will not be stilled, although to that which refuses Its blessing, It may appear as a "chastening rod." *The truth of our being will not ever let us rest comfortably in that which is less than Soul's beauty, grace, harmony, holiness, and perfection.* When we try to settle for the ego counterfeits to spiritual, quality good, we will inevitably end up feeling betrayed. It is not God, or good, that has betrayed us, but our misconception of the good. Problems, as Hora clarifies, are "lessons designed for our edification." They point us ever higher to the spiritual foundation upon which all real goodness is based.

Joseph Campbell writes:

> In Buddhist systems, more especially those of Tibet, the med-
> itation Buddhas appear in two aspects, one peaceful and the
> other wrathful. If you are clinging fiercely to your ego and its
> little temporal world of sorrows and joys, hanging on for dear
> life, it will be the wrathful aspect of the deity that appears.
> It will seem terrifying. But the moment your ego yields and
> gives up, that same meditation Buddha is experienced as the
> bestower of bliss.[15]

Ultimately, Buddha represents the divine nature of all being. Bud-dha nature is Soul identity, and, as Campbell describes, ego's reaction to Soul awareness may be fear and heightened self-confirmation. But as we realize that our inner turmoil arises at the initiative of Soul, we can cooperate with the process of ego-yielding rather than fighting it.

There are ultimately no such things as "anti-Soul forces," even though it may seem that way to us. What seems to assault the best in ourselves and others isn't on the level of Soul at all. It is the misconception of located mind and life operating mechanically, not intentionally, to confirm itself in the face of that which would dissolve it. In the New Testament, the writer of the letter to the Hebrews describes "the removal of what is shaken, as of what has been made, in order that what cannot be shaken may remain." He then adds, "Therefore let us be grateful for receiving a kingdom that cannot be shaken, and thus let us offer to God acceptable worship, with reverence and awe; for our God is a consuming fire" (Heb. 12:27–29, RSV).

Despite the disturbances that seem to interrupt the uncovering of our Soul identity and Its blissful awareness, Soul is the fact and ego is the misconception about that fact. There is nothing other than qual-ity Life taking place, anywhere. Nothing can stop the awareness of that reality from shining through the mists of personal sense with increasing clarity.

Soul Seeing Reports

The experience of a British officer, Major Haswell, who was serving in Belgium during World War II, took place in the most dramatic setting and had the most substantial effects on the human scene of any I have read about. At the time of the realization, he and his artillery unit were pinned down by German fire in a Belgian farmyard. He wrote:

> The scene was like Dante's Inferno with the shells coming in one after another and exploding about 3 feet above the ground, which made us crouch down in the slit trench....I now received an enquiry why I had not moved and, after explaining the situation, was given a direct order to move at once.
>
> I turned to the men with me and said, "We have to move, and I don't think any of us will live in this....I am going to say a prayer, and I would advise you to make peace with God in your own way." The noise about us was deafening,...and we expected to be cut to pieces as we emerged from the shelter of the slit trench....
>
> As soon as I said "Amen," I blew my whistle to signal the gun tractor up, and shouted "let's go" at the same time scrambling out of the slit trench.... *Then something happened.*
>
> The moment I stood upright the sound of the shells exploding ceased, but I still saw the flame of the explosions. But now there was a stillness, and I could hear the song of birds, loud and quite close. (There were no birds within miles of the farm!) Then I saw fluttering and hovering on the dung heap at the side of the gun, a white cabbage butterfly. (I am sure there were no butterflies either!)...
>
> Then I became aware as it were, instantaneously, that I was now in the field, in front of the farm, and all was peace, no sound, no flames, nothing, only the field, the sun, the trees and the sound of many birds trilling.
>
> Suddenly...I was at the bottom of many blades of grass... all pulsing, thrusting upwards but exulting in a form of soundless praise...alive and in tune with the Universe of which they formed a part....

In an instant all changed. I was running forward immediately from the edge of the slit trench, my men clambering out behind me!...I assisted the men to move the gun and ammunition limber into position for hook-up. Whilst this was in process the shells were still actually exploding about us! When the tractor arrived the canvas top was hit by shrapnel.

During all this chaos one event remains vividly in my memory. It was one of the gun team on the opposite side of the tractor to me shouting "It's a bloody miracle!" We hooked up and proceeded to the head of the 6 gun column. Not a single man had received as much as a scratch,... We were fired on as we proceeded down the roadway to our destination, not a vehicle or gun being hit.[16]

This is an awesome report, and one that warrants close examination so that we may understand what happened as evidence of universal consciousness laws that are as available to us as they were to Major Haswell. It was a miracle from the human perspective, but, like all miracles, it illustrated higher realities and laws rather than being a random or arbitrary violation of physical law produced by a personal God. This report both clarifies the nature of what we are calling Soul and Its seeing, and also suggests how the shift from ego eyes to Soul eyes may take place.

Spiritual reality is timeless, and timelessness is illustrated by the fact that, according to the bombardier's report afterward, Major Haswell had never halted long enough for any such experience to have occurred. After jumping out of the slit trench he had just kept running on to the gun, not pausing until he had reached it. Time is, then, revealed to be an arbitrary designation of material sense rather than a fact of divine consciousness.

Likewise, our sense of space and what fills it is demolished by this report. Of stunning impact is the evidence that right where the material, personal level of thought is experiencing "Dante's Inferno," Soul is seeing and being "heaven." The stillness, sense of peace, sound of birds trilling, vision of sunlight, and a fluttering butterfly took place in the same "space" as the screaming hell of explosions, flame, cordite, flying dung, and dying cattle.

Getting Kicked Out of Ego

Greatly intriguing to me is the question of what went on in Major Haswell's consciousness that allowed Soul to dominate not only his own awareness but the whole field of activity. When I read the report, one of the things that struck me was his unquestioned obedience to the command to move out. With a true soldier's discipline, duty took precedence over personal needs, even unto death. It would seem that Major Haswell, in effect, died to his ego the moment he accepted the order. The horror of the scene, coupled with his acceptance of the order to stand up in the very midst of it, effectively "kicked him out" of his ego sense. He acted from that moment on out of a higher, ego-detached sense of identity that was much nearer Soul than ego.

Finally, since consciousness really is universal rather than located, Major Haswell's release of his own located sense, and subsequent frolic in the Soul universe, served to depersonalize the whole mental scene enough for Soul awareness to operate as the protection of his men and equipment. Anybody who knows the Psalm 91 ought not stand aghast at this report. Doesn't the psalm promise that "he that dwelleth in the secret place of the most High shall abide under the shadow of the Almighty"? While "a thousand shall fall at thy side, and ten thousand at thy right hand...it shall not come nigh thee....For he shall give his angels charge over thee, to keep thee in all thy ways." Maybe this isn't just pretty poetry!

Arthur Koestler, as a writer and thinker, is able to analyze his bliss experience conceptually. In doing this, he provides some clues to Major Haswell's experience as well as to his own. While languishing in a Spanish prison awaiting execution, Koestler was scratching on the wall with a piece of wire. He reconfirmed for himself Euclid's premise that the number of prime numbers is infinite. He wrote:

> The significance of this swept over me like a wave. The wave had originated in an articulate verbal insight; but this evaporated at once, leaving in its wake only a wordless essence, a fragrance of eternity, a quiver of the arrow in the blue. I must have stood there some minutes, entranced, with a wordless awareness that "this is perfect—perfect"; until I noticed some

slight mental discomfort nagging at the back of my mind —
some trivial circumstance that marred the perfection of the
moment. Then I remembered the nature of that irrelevant annoyance: *I* was of course in prison and might be shot. But this
was immediately answered by a feeling whose verbal translation would be: "So what? Is that all? Have you got nothing
more serious to worry about?" — an answer so spontaneous,
fresh and amused as if the intruding annoyance had been the
loss of a collar-stud. Then I was floating on my back in a
river of peace, under bridges of silence.... The I had ceased
to exist....

When I say "the I had ceased to exist" I refer to a con-
crete experience [whose] primary mark is the sensation that
this state is more real that any other one has experienced before — that for the first time the veil has fallen and one is
in touch with "real reality," the hidden order of things, the
X-ray texture of the world, normally obscured by layers of
irrelevancy....

These experiences filled me with a direct certainty that
a higher order of reality existed, and that it alone invested
existence with meaning.[17]

Koestler's report reveals how insignificant a sense of personal identity is within the larger universal awareness. If even being shot is of
such little importance in divine reality, how much less significant are
the details of daily ego living that so captivate our thinking! This testimony often reminds me of the need to shift from ego eyes to Soul
eyes when I seem stuck on some personal issue. Why continue to let
"irrelevancy" block my awareness of the "really real" substance of Life?
Why continue to seek and starve for meaning on a level of seeing that
is itself inherently meaningless?

We will never either make sense of "evil" or overcome it from a personal standpoint. But as spiritual discernment reveals to us the "gifts of
God" we find our experience reflecting that goodness more and more
consistently. The knowledge of Soul identity releases us from the experiences of "the natural man" and enables us to claim for others their
Soul integrity as well.

CHAPTER 4

Soul Relationships

The special love relationship is the ego's chief weapon for keeping you from Heaven.

—A COURSE IN MIRACLES[18]

The great thing is to have lots of love *about*. I don't see...that it matters who loves as long as somebody does....It's a great thing...to get on with one's loving. Perhaps you can tell me of anything else in the world that works such wonders.

—LOTTY WILKINS IN *The Enchanted April*[19]

God is love; and he that dwelleth in love dwelleth in God, and God in him.

—1 JOHN 4:16

Romantic love continues to be the ideal in our society. Most popular songs deal with the promise and/or the disappointments of romance. Probably every human being has had the experience of romantic attraction. It feels like the most wonderful thing in the world. On the other hand, there is an edge to it that isn't so wonderful. One man, recalling his teenage romantic spasms, said that they came over him like the flu. His thought became obsessed with the object of the moment. He felt sick with the infatuation and felt "blind," that is, oblivious to everything but fantasies of the beloved.

The intensity of love for a particular person is the hallmark of personal romantic love. It is entirely object-oriented, and that's the problem. The lover sees in the object of his or her attraction a possibility for self-completion and self-love that seems impossible on his or her own. Romantic love says, "Because I love (empower) you, your love of me can make me feel good and worthy and whole and happy with myself." The focus is upon the object as specially equipped to give the lover a sense of value and well-being, but that is only because the lover's ego has thus empowered the beloved.

The Subject, Not the Object, of Love

In reality, the important thing in a love relationship is the *subject*, not the *object*, of the love. Love is a subjective reality, not an objective one. Soul love appears as the love of seeing loveliness and of being loving rather than the love of some particular person. Of course, the romantic belief is that the object of love can give the lover the capacity to love. But that implies that the beloved's behavior can likewise deprive the lover of the lover's lovingness. No person can bear the weight of such seeming power. *Romantic love makes a false god of the beloved, and false gods always turn into devils.* The fleeting, euphoric sense of self-worth bestowed by requited romantic love quickly flips into depression or rage as the object fails to fulfill the lover's ego expectations.

Love is an attribute of God and belongs to our spiritual, not our human, identity. We either discover Soul, and with It a lasting, unshakeable sense of Self-love and lovingness, or we do not. But interpersonal relationships do not and cannot take the place of Soul discovery. Although the chapter is titled "Soul Relationships," in fact, Soul does not relate, because in Soul we are in oneness with all, and it is *out from* this oneness that harmonious human participation takes place.

A Course in Miracles points to this fact in the quotation that opened this chapter. "The special love relationship," which is the Course's name for romantic love, "is the ego's chief weapon for keeping you from Heaven" because heaven, as we have been discovering, is the state of consciousness that occurs when we see from Soul's rather than ego's standpoint. The moment we abandon our Soul center within, we have abandoned heaven; we have cast ourselves into the hell of separate existence, and there is no help for it within that state or level of consciousness.

Marianne Williamson writes,

Our desire to find one "special person," one part of the Sonship who will complete us, is hurtful because it is delusional. It means we're seeking salvation in separation rather than in oneness. The only love that completes us is the love of God, and the love of God is the love of everyone....

Often when we think we are "in love" with a person ... we're actually anything but.... A special relationship is a relationship based on fear ... [and] guilt. The special relationship is the ego's seductive pull away from God. It is a major form of idolatry, or temptation to think that something other than God can complete us and give us peace....

The purpose of a relationship is not for two incomplete people to become one, but rather for two complete people to join together for the greater glory of God.[20]

It always helps to know *what* something is before we ask *how* to do or fix it. In defining the purpose of a relationship as "two complete people" joining together for the glory of God, Williamson shifts relationships from the ego level to the Soul level. Egos, by definition, are not and never will be complete; Soul, in contrast, designates our already complete, divine identity. So, what the Course calls "a holy relationship" we understand to be Soul completeness expressed as harmonious companionship and love.

Joint Participation in the Good of God

Thomas Hora defines marriage as "joint participation in the good of God." This clarifies the holy foundation of a Soul-based togetherness. The commitment is not to person but to "the good of God," which is not other than the good of one's own true being. There is no essential self-betrayal at the heart of this marriage commitment. Therefore, attention is not continually being captivated by self-and-other issues.

Years ago a very minor incident became a major discovery of what "joint participation" means. Jan and I were spending a weekend at a hotel in Connecticut, which I, as a matter of course, felt we could not afford. Tommy was a toddler, and I felt very busy with my self-appointed task of managing-the-scene-with-too-few-resources.

At breakfast, Tommy ordered pancakes, which he then spurned in favor of my toast. I was feeling robbed of my little supply of toast and was trying to make him eat the pancakes that he had ordered. Jan, sensing my distress, offered him a piece of his toast. I burst out, "Oh, Jan, don't let him take your toast too!" Jan replied, "Sweetheart, there isn't 'your' toast and 'my' toast. There's just toast. And if we need more we can order it."

Of course! How could I have been so upset about nothing! The simplicity and clarity of this statement punctured the spell of my self-imposed distress like a pin in a balloon. I felt like a fool, but a very relieved and grateful fool. He could so easily have just become annoyed with me: "For Pete's sake, woman, stop your fussing!" I couldn't have blamed him. But instead, he spoke the truth, in the most relevant way. He wasn't just talking about toast. What I became aware of as he spoke was: "There isn't a 'yours' and a 'mine.' There's only Life. And if we need more of some form of It, we can 'order' It from the Source."

"Ordering" Self-Respect

Self-respect is something nearly everybody needs and wants more of, but when we try to get it from others, we respect ourselves even less for the effort. Ordering self-respect may seem harder than ordering toast, but it is just as readily available if we know where to place the order. Self-respect belongs to Soul identity. Ego identity seeks and doesn't find respect for itself because it is not respectable. It is, by definition, a sense of limitation and lack that needs to be relinquished rather than respected.

In the toast episode, I got supplied with more than toast in the recognition that the way I was seeing what was going on was totally off-base. I was seeing "yours" and "mine" and therefore feeling vulnerable to the moods and whims of others. The minute we think that our well-being is *derived from* others, we are fearful of being *deprived by* others. Then we can't help turning into anxious fusspots, trying to make our children and spouses and parents and friends fit into our plans. And a sense of self-respect eludes us.

We order self-respect, not from other selves, but from God. We place the order by going within, to our Soul center, and looking to see the situation through Soul eyes. If you think that this sounds too idealistic, consider the following dialogue that took place recently between two men in their early twenties. One fellow was very depressed because his long-term girlfriend had finally dumped him due to his repeated infidelities. He couldn't understand what he did to deserve such total rejection. "After all," he said, "I didn't ever *intend* to cheat on her, and she knows that. It's not like I went out looking for somebody else. Why can't she understand that?"

A buddy of the man who was bemoaning his fate then took him to task. "Maybe you don't intend to cheat, but every time you go out without your girlfriend, cheating is a possibility for you. That's because your reason for not cheating is that your girlfriend won't like it. And if she hasn't been very nice to you that day or there's a really sexy chick who comes on to you, you think, 'Why not? It's okay as long as she doesn't find out.'

"You need to decide this on a different basis. You need to consider what kind of a man you want to be. You need to ask yourself if you want your word to mean anything, if you want others to respect you as somebody who keeps his commitments. And this doesn't just apply to relationships either. It applies to everything in your life: your job, your friendships, everything.

"If you decide you want to be a man worthy of respect, whose word means what he says, then when you go to a party, there isn't anything to think about or decide. You know before you go in that, having given your word to your girlfriend, there's no possibility of connecting with another girl that night. And if you decide you want to break the commitment, then you tell your girlfriend up front that the relationship is over before you start going out with others."

The buddy's advice is Soul wisdom in action. It correctly identifies the issue as the man's inner integrity rather than pleasing the girlfriend. The latter motive keeps one a child. The desire to please is always coupled with a desire to rebel in order to prove one's "freedom." But when we get clear with ourselves what *we* want our lives to be about, then we stand on an inner rock of certainty, from which self-respect and respect of others take place without thought. From that Soul foundation, we find support and direction, not only in our relationships, but in all of our activities and affairs.

An Exorcism of Blame

Soul leads us to pay attention to the spiritual substance of things and let that shape and harmonize the human forms. In considering relationship issues, then, it is important to start from a point beyond self and others. *If we truly desire quality relationships, then we will need to be more interested in quality than in relationships.* The ego is always interested in relationships and never interested in quality, because it is interested in itself, and therefore in other selves. It is always looking to see whether it is getting what it wants from others and judging others on that basis. And blame is therefore endemic to the field of personal relationships.

Blame would keep us reliving the most horrific ego pain for the sake of pointing to a personal cause, declaring another person to be wrong and bad, and insisting, implicitly, that that person be punished. In blaming, we pay a terrible, ongoing price in order to keep pointing the finger.

A woman who was in her forties complained about her ongoing problem with her now-aged mother. The mother had physically abused the woman when she was a very small child. The woman said, "Every time I am with my mother I want to make her acknowledge and apologize for abusing me. I've been trying to make her do that for years, but she just won't recognize what she did."

I replied, "It's good that you have faced the hurt yourself and that you have brought it out into the open with your mother. But what you find is that your mother is incapable of responding in the way that you want. It's bad enough that the abuse happened once. But every time you mentally rehearse it for the purpose of blaming your mother, you do it to yourself again. This is self-abuse. Isn't it time to stop repeating it?"

The woman was stunned. "Nobody ever told me that before," she said. "It never occurred to me that *I* was keeping the sense of abuse going, or that there was something I could do *in my own thinking* to make it stop."

If we would be free from the pain, a first step is to recognize that the problems we have encountered are not the fault of other people. Nor are we to blame personally. The fault lies in the initial human belief of separation that then invites us to try to get wholeness from others who themselves suffer from the hurtful, human misconception. This is an impossible goal from the start. It's like trying to get sunshine from another person. The fault is not in the other but in the expectation.

Dancing to the Soundless Music of Life

When we put spiritual values first in our thinking, Soul not only directs our activity but attracts others who share the values and the vision. And what other foundation for relationships could really work? How could we even want to be involved with others if they do not resonate with our highest values and interests, and we with theirs?

Hora likens joint participation in the good of God to ballroom dancers. He writes:

> Let us suppose that two people decided to dance together without music. In this case one individual would of necessity impose his ideas upon the other and force him (or her) to move according to his will. This is analogous to interpersonal relationships. This would... be arduous, pushing one another around, stepping on one another's toes.
>
> But when two good dancers dance together to music, what happens? It is a joint participation in the rhythmic impulses which the music imposes upon them. They respond harmoniously and gracefully. It is the music that governs the dancers and the dance.
>
> We thus realize that dancing cannot be done; a good dancer does not do the dancing. A good dancer allows the music to dance him, so to speak. When the soundless music of life is heard, then the will of God governs man in supreme wisdom, love and grace. To hear the soundless music of life is a great blessing and freedom, it means living in grace. And that is also an aspect of the good of God.[21]

Referring back to the dialogue between the two young men, we can see that we "dance to the soundless music of life" by going within, not by going without. We consult our highest, *subjective* sense of value. So we do not get caught in the tension of trying to meet an external standard that we then are driven to rebel against.

The Soul Principle

It's important not to confuse Soul's vision with ego's fantasy. If a couple is to dance harmoniously, it must be to Life's music, not a rhythm imposed by one of the partners. Many couple problems aren't *couple* problems at all. Rather, one of the partners has an ego-based picture of what marriage or family is supposed to be and tries to make the partner, the children, even him/herself fit the picture. When that attempt goes bankrupt, blame is spread around to all the participants. The real offender — the insistence of an ego fantasy — is not even noticed.

As a marriage counselor, I have heard scores of people complain that after marriage they found their spouse to be "just like" their father or mother or previous spouse, even though they had consciously tried to avoid such a choice and had thought that this individual was totally different. No counselor is going to be the least bit surprised by such claims. If we let personal fantasies choose our partners, we can be assured that we will end up with reruns of our personal identity issues. It is obviously futile at that point to try to fix the fantasy by trying to make the other people be different.

The Soul principle in relationships is that *problems are seen to lie in one's own thinking, not in the thinking or behavior of the other.* We keep our attention upon what is claiming to be our own viewpoint rather than on another's personality. But this is not a matter of trying to change ourselves instead of trying to change others. We cannot change our ego identity and values directly. For years I envied and wished I could become another Terry Cole Whittaker or Marianne Williamson, but I just couldn't. As a person, I can only be Ann. But I've gotten to be a much happier and freer Ann as I've been able to honor my Soul identity. I am much less determined by comparisons with others and much more able to stand with my own best sense of what is right for me.

Being guided from within our Soul center — in Maslow's terms, our "intrinsic conscience" — we find that Soul's universal values operate as a kind of quality control in consciousness. Shifts in our sense of ourselves and of what is good and right for us take place spontaneously. Inevitably, such shifts influence how we evaluate our activities and relationships. Things we used to do and the people we used to do them with may become unsatisfying and even be recognized as troublesome when seen in the light of higher values.

Each of us is determined, more than we can imagine, by values that belong to family beliefs. These are very difficult to notice with any distance, because they are just part of the ego scene. They are invisible family heirlooms that go unrecognized unless and until we find and cherish other values that can call such ego values into question.

The values of Soul, as revealed in bliss reports, include beauty, joy, harmony, wholeness, love, wonder, inherent value, and peace. Even though as persons we may not be able to appreciate Soul values, we know that they are good. They will never betray us as other people are bound to do. And it is only in Soul that we can avoid betraying others.

Seeing through the Spoiler's Act

Strangely, it is often our loved ones who get the least of our spiritual attention. We are so ego-involved with their egos that we don't often think to draw back and consider them through Soul eyes. I have found that often before I can do that I need to recognize and deal with the operation of "the spoiler." I learned the effectiveness of this a few years ago.

After Jan had gone to the office one morning, I found myself ruminating about some comments he had made at breakfast. They had annoyed me greatly, and I began to tell him off mentally. I puttered around the house, babbling to myself like a madwoman, muttering imprecations, dredging up every item on my grudge list from the moment we met. At last the stream of accusations dried up, and a single thought stood out: "Thank God I didn't say any of those things to him. They are not true."

At that moment a picture of Jan came to mind. It could be called my Soul picture of him. It is a special image of him at his best, his face shining and open, his generosity and sweetness and humor beaming forth. That's my Jan, my beloved husband, my Soul partner. I could suddenly see that the things I was reacting to were all aspects of the spoiler sense that he hated as much as I. He would never choose the thoughts and feelings that had captivated him at breakfast.

So I began to tell off the spoiler instead. I walked around, addressing it out loud: "You lousy spoiler, you don't belong to me or my Life. You cannot masquerade as my husband or as any other aspect of my experience. God is my Mind and my Life and that of Jan too. You have no place here." And so on. When that was finished, I got on with my work and thought no more of the episode. At lunch, Jan came in announcing, "I can't explain it, but I feel so happy." I blurted out, "Well, I can explain it. I kicked the shit out of the spoiler this morning." Jan looked at me in shock, and we both burst out laughing. Ever since then, when he feels himself getting stuck, he'll invite me to help him "kick the shit out of the spoiler."

Our loved ones are not what ego — theirs or ours — says they are. When we love them enough to separate the truth of them from the ego voice and picture, we are the first ones to profit. The more we really love to see from a spiritual quality standpoint, the easier it gets to see through ego claims.

The shift from an external, interpersonal orientation and agenda to one deriving from our Soul integrity brings about subtle changes in our existing relationships. At first these changes may feel uncomfortable to us and to those with whom we have been playing out ego dramas. A psychologist and his wife told of how aggravating it was to her when he began to discover a spiritual orientation to issues. They had had a pattern of fighting over disagreements. The husband began to understand that he needed to work out his problems first in his own thinking, so he wouldn't immediately engage interpersonally anymore. This made his wife feel anxious and at sea. The frustration of her old pattern of managing her feelings by interpersonal combat led to a period of heightened adversarialness on her part. She would try every provocation she could come up with to get her husband "into the ring" with her. But eventually, as she noticed that he was actually getting free from some of his problems, she became interested in learning what he was learning.

Marianne Williamson writes:

> The ego seeks to use a relationship to fill our needs as we define them; the Holy Spirit asks that the relationship be used by God to serve His purposes. And His purpose is always that we might learn how to love others more purely. We love purely when we release other people to be who they are. The ego seeks intimacy through control and guilt. The Holy Spirit seeks intimacy through acceptance and release.

> In the holy relationship, we don't seek to change someone, but rather to see how beautiful they already are....A holy relationship is this: "a common state of mind, where both give errors gladly to correction, that both may happily be healed as one."[22]

What the Course calls "a holy relationship" is not something the ego can achieve. It helps greatly to know that Soul takes care of making our relationships holy as we keep our attention centered in Soul values and qualities.

"Neither Married Nor Not Married"

I was thirty-four years old when I married. For years I had despaired of ever marrying, believing myself not attractive enough to marry. My explorations in psychotherapy had revealed a deep-seated fear of marriage, based upon what I saw as my mother's entrapment and unhappiness as a wife and mother. Yet I felt consciously that marriage was essential to my happiness.

When I began my training analysis with Dr. Hora, the issue of marriage was one of the first things that his existential-spiritual approach illuminated for me. He said, "Whether you marry or do not marry, you are always alone with God. The enlightened man is neither married nor not married." This made me aware that marriage was not an existential issue, not something absolutely determining my life. I understood that my destiny and well-being lay in my consciousness of the divine Life, and that I had to work that out with God, whether I was married or not.

The relief was enormous. The unbearable weight of believing that marriage could either ruin or save my life was lifted. Having said, only a few weeks earlier, that I didn't even know an eligible man, I looked around the same scene and noticed four eligible men. The situation hadn't changed; my mentality had.

At the end of the first year of training, I came home for vacation. I was talking with an old friend, and I remarked to her that for the first time in my life my best friend was a man. I was referring to Jan, who less than a year later became my husband. The connection between

forming a deep friendship with Jan and marriage to him was not incidental. Like many single adults, I tended to evaluate every "available"
man as a potential mate. The relationship was then, from the start,
charged with all the ambivalence of my inner conflicts about marriage.
I couldn't relax and be real, nor could I see the man as he was. Realizing
that marriage was incidental to, rather than central to, my happiness
and well-being released me from that dreadful spell, which plagues so
many single adults in our society.

There have been storms of individual disturbance for each of us
through the years. We think that our capacity to weather these storms
lies in our mutual commitment to building a quality life together,
based on our highest understanding of God and spiritual reality. That
commitment has given us maximum room for individual growth and
change with a minimum focus on getting the behavior our egos might
like from each other. Most important, it has enabled each of us to stay
out of the other's struggles by not taking the other's behavior personally. Then we have been able to be supportive and encouraging partners
against the common adversary of human beliefs.

Sex and Values

Sexually transmitted diseases, relationship disharmonies, rampant sexual violence, abuse and harassment, and the emotional pain of sexual
identity confusion are evidences that the current sexual beliefs, values,
and attitudes are badly askew in our culture. Ego sex is totally devoid
of values. The ego's inescapable drive for self-confirmation leads it to
pursue an essentially amoral agenda. It wants what it wants when it
wants it, even if what it wants is self-destructive. There is no inherent
standard of values within personal ego sense.

Human discussion focuses on *behaviors* as "right" or "wrong" when
it is not the physical but the mental activity that is crucial to our
safety and well-being. Sex is no different from anything else in our
experience. Letting ego determine our behavior guarantees that our
experience will be characterized by the dualism and limitation that
belong to personal identity. Letting Soul and Its values be expressed
as our behavior sanctifies the behavior, keeping it wholesome and
life-enhancing.

The so-called sex drive is not a physiological given, as is assumed by many people. Most people observe for themselves that their inclination toward sexual activity varies according to a number of nonphysical issues, including the behavior of the partner, the presence or absence of other people, babies, job pressures, and just plain moods.

It is the meaning of the sexual activity to the ego that determines the extent of the "drive" and accounts for the preferred forms of activity. Rather than being important aspects of our individuality and integrity, sexual proclivities represent unchosen, usually unexamined, beliefs that claim to be our personal identity. Instead of blindly embracing those arbitrary beliefs and letting them drive our behavior, for good or ill, we have the option of examining the beliefs to see whether they are truthful and life-affirming.

If you want to identify the meaning of sexual activity to you, you can do so by paying attention to your sexual fantasies. What is taking place in fantasy? What is the interpersonal situation? Are you exerting power over another, being dominated, demeaning or being demeaned, hurting or being hurt? Or is the mental climate appreciative, sweet, affectionate? No pleasure is worth being bought at the price of an unwholesome mentality, because that distorted sense of yourself and others will play out in self-defeating ways in other aspects of your life.

The Meaning of Attraction

Whether an individual finds himself or herself sexually attracted to an individual of the same or of the opposite sex, the basic meaning is the same. The object of the attraction is perceived to "contain" qualities that the lover is drawn to possess or be possessed by, or the act of possession satisfies a perceived ego need in some way. The psychological meanings of sexuality are individual and therefore almost infinitely varied.

For example, Hora reports on the following meaning of a young man's homosexuality:

> A young man became a homosexual to the great consternation of his respectable parents. Yet when the situation was

explored, it was revealed that the boy was striving to live up to his parents' exaggerated concern with the importance of being masculine, beyond any suspicion of showing so-called "sissy" tendencies. To this boy, homosexuality was a way of "practicing" what his parents "preached": he was asserting his own masculinity over other, less "masculine" males.[23]

Another example involves a heterosexual man, to whom sexual activity was a preoccupying interest, and who considered himself and was considered by many women to be "a very sexy guy." He was astonished to discover that at base his drive was a little boy's hunger to be close to his mother. Raised by a very demanding father with a mother who wasn't particularly interested in him, he was plagued by the desire to retreat from his father's demands into his mother's arms. But, of course, a strong male doesn't let himself know that he "wants his mommie"! It's entirely acceptable, however, to be "a horny guy."

Actually, I think that the "horniness" of many "macho" or hard-driving, ambitious men is a manifestation of their longing for the softer, feminine qualities with which their self-image refuses to allow them to identify. Their ego denial of the feminine aspects of their own being takes form as an insatiable hunger for sexual oneness with female persons.

Orgasm as Ego Transcendence

For all of us, then, our sexual attractions are not what they seem on the surface. They involve psychological issues that in turn point to ultimate issues of identity, love, and wholeness, which require Soul solutions. We are in pursuit of something more than orgasm when we pursue orgasm. We are, ultimately, in pursuit of our own completeness and holiness.

The activity leading to orgasm is determined, as we have seen, by ego beliefs. But ultimately, the pleasure of orgasm lies in release from the tight boundaries of body/ego identity. It provides a fleeting experience of ego transcendence. The more one is identified with the body, the more important its sensations seem. To that level of thought, orgasm may provide virtually the only moment of ego-release available. It therefore assumes exaggerated importance, and the need for repetition may even become compulsive.

Orgasm is essentially tension release, and the greater the tension, the more pleasurable the release. But the price of the pleasure is incessant tension. The very emphasis on physical sensation is the problem, not the solution, since it operates to restrict awareness to the most material, hence limiting, level of thought. A preoccupation with pornography reveals just such a constriction of consciousness. The restrictiveness of a focus on genital organs so screens out the quality dimensions of life that it heightens the sense of entrapment and the desperate drive for release. This is an obsessive, circular pattern in which, like all addictive behavior, the "solution" becomes a greater problem than the initial problem.

In the quest for transcendence, orgasm is one of the greatest betrayers. Its ecstasy is so conditional and fleeting that, like drugs and other material means of mental release, it invites compulsion and abuse. If it's transcendence we are really after, then it's better to know that and seek it where it may profoundly and lastingly be found, in a shift from physical to spiritual identity.

Needs of Young People

Adolescents and young adults need time and permission to sort out their feelings and experiences according to their developing values and maturing identity sense. There are sexual dimensions to attractions that are really quality based and that need to be kept quality oriented. Attractions, such as to role models and mentors, should be able to take place without our assuming that our sexual identity is involved. I remember having a terrific crush on a nun with whom I worked when I was in my early twenties. She was a very beautiful and dynamic woman, and I admired her and wanted to be like her. It never occurred to me to consider my feelings as related to "sexual preference," so the relationship remained enhancing and trouble-free.

As I considered the issue of sex and teenagers for a previous book, the following thoughts came to mind:

It is not nearly so important for teens to know what is wrong, harmful, and dangerous as for them to know what is right, good, beautiful, true. It is our awareness of the qualities of Life that sorts through the possibilities and temptations that confront us and determines what we end up considering to be good and thus choosing. Knowing something of the real Good, our kids are not nearly so vulnerable to the supposed goods of teen society. If we would fill our schools with qualities education — that is, education in the qualities of real Life — as well as teaching the facts about sex and drugs, teenagers would be less likely to grab for self-destructive goodies out of an ignorance of where true satisfaction lies.[24]

Sexual Miseducation

Watching TV and movies with our sons over the past decade, I have been appalled to see how many scenes of sexual intercourse occur. Total nudity, which can be shown in a nonprurient way, is not permitted in R-rated movies. Yet as long as body parts are not shown, the positions and gyrations of sexual intercourse are routinely thrown in. What a peculiar standard! My objection to this, not only for teens and young adults but for us all, is based upon the direct and destructive miseducation that takes place in this way.

First of all, these scenes are almost always prurient in intent, that is, included purely for the titillation of the audience. While the rationale is that viewers like to be sexually aroused and will pay money for it, that very fact reveals a cultural belief that needs to be examined. It is the belief that sexual activity, hence arousal, is good in itself. This belief is widely promulgated, and it is mistaken. The physiology of sex is not inherently valuable. It just is. "Birds do it, bees do it..." When people do it, the activity has the value that the *mentalities* of the participants bring to it. It may be loving, considerate, intelligent, etc., or it may be degrading and mentally and morally crippling, even if it is consensual.

Second, the implicit message in these repetitive scenes of intercourse is that if one is even mildly interested in another person, sexual intercourse is the first and ultimate mode of expressing this interest. It appears to be the prime way of getting acquainted! Everything else in a relationship is secondary and of lesser value. Thus, the real, quality stuff of a meaningful relationship — the mutuality of shared interests, affection, respect, sensitivity, and values — is discredited. Far from enhancing a relationship, immediate sex tends to stunt the growth of those quality aspects that constitute the substance of it.

Third, the entire culture has been trained in voyeurism. When I was training as a psychotherapist, being a voyeur was considered to be a sickness. Getting sexual kicks out of watching other people "do it" was classified as a sexual perversion. No longer is this the case. While it may be a good idea not to label and condemn behaviors as "sick" or "perverted," I think an important recognition has been lost. It is the recognition that valuable sex is private sex. The Soul of sex lies in its being the most intimate expression between two people of their love, affection, respect for, and enjoyment of each other. There is a kind of rape involved in exposing something precious and private to the gawking eyes of spectators. The quality is violated and corrupted. It should not surprise us that rape has become commonplace in our society.

Looking at sexuality from a consciousness standpoint gives us a fresh take on the knotty problems of that aspect of human experience. What happens in consciousness becomes the all-important issue. A preoccupation with sex is a problem, even if behavior looks entirely "proper," because any and all material, personal preoccupations shutter the windows of Soul, keeping us identified with and vulnerable to all the limitations and plagues of human ego belief. Our culture is broadly impacted by the horrors of mindless, loveless, Soulless physical couplings, and the fog of a pornographic mental focus.

Soul Identity and Sex

Starting from Soul, we find our beliefs about sexuality illuminated and changed. Soul identity is already whole, and it includes all of the masculine and feminine qualities of being. We are, as a culture, increasingly aware that "real men" and "real women" include a balance of masculine and feminine qualities, and that the gender stereotypes of macho men and subservient women rob us of our spiritual right to the fullness of our being.

From the ultimate level of Soul identity, there is no such thing as a sexual or gender identity. There is only spiritual identity, which is neither heterosexual nor homosexual; it is complete and whole. Reasoning from this standpoint, we can see that sexual preferences are not absolutely fixed, whether from genetic, psychological, or divine causes. An individual's particular sexual propensities are "given" and "fixed" only within that ego's identity sense. The shift to Soul identity brings about a reframing of viewpoint which may show up in remarkable shifts of feeling and interest. "With God, all things are possible." The more we pay attention to the qualities of spiritual identity, which is the only real identity, the more our sexual proclivities per se, lose importance in our thinking and reflect increasingly the love, intelligence, harmony, and health of real Life. To repeat and paraphrase: *If we want to have quality sex, we need to be more interested in quality than in sex.*

The poet Percy Shelley wrote of "Love's Philosophy":

> See the mountains kiss high Heaven
> And the waves clasp one another;
> No sister-flower would be forgiven
> If it disdained its brother;
> And the sunlight clasps the earth
> And the moonbeams kiss the sea:
> What are all these kissings worth
> If thou kiss not me?

The answer is: Everything! All these kissings are worth everything! In the seeing of them, we are kissed by Soul awareness, and Soul's kiss is heaven, here and now. From this awareness can come many human kisses, but it does not work the other way around.

Soul Seeing Reports

The following report shared with me by a friend illustrates the power of Soul's kiss to heal human discord and lovelessness:

> At the time, personal relations in our home were strained. For several months we had been trying to do something about the situation, but the tension continued. Then one evening

an unusual thing occurred which completely changed the atmosphere.

I was sitting in the living room in a big chair facing the front window and the pine trees outside.... I felt a great desire to put my misery behind me — all its selfishness, pride, and fear. It was not worth holding on to. Mentally I put it down, let go of the whole weight of it.

Almost immediately something extraordinary began to happen. A special vibrancy filled the air. I became completely absorbed in this feeling of vibrant aliveness. It was as though the universe had a rhythm of its own which was suddenly making itself felt....

In addition to the vibrant atmosphere, I was particularly aware of the trees outside the window. There was a light breeze blowing, and the pine boughs were moving to the same rhythm as that inside the room. At the same time, there was a special light, a sort of glow, on the boughs of the trees. This combination of movement, rhythm and light was ecstatically beautiful....

All of a sudden my husband, who had been in the basement, appeared in the doorway of the living room and said, "Do you feel that?" I said, "Yes." He sat down on the couch next to the window and also looked out.... He sat there for quite a while, not speaking.

I had the feeling that I must get out of doors, near the trees, to touch them. By this time, it was dark, and there was no place to walk near our house. So I got into the car and drove to a section of town where there were sidewalks. The street where I stopped was lined with big trees, old massive oaks and elms.... These trees were just as alive as the pine trees at home. Their boughs were also moving quietly, gently, to a soothing rhythm. They were expressing love toward me, and I was filled with love for them. Love was everywhere, the presence of Love felt as Life, substance, energy, a vibrant energy so beautiful that it cannot be put into words....

This experience revolutionized our lives. We began to live in harmony, in impersonal oneness. Problems that had been bothersome simply faded away. They were not important any more. The discords of a petty, limited sense of existence no longer claimed our attention. We were able to live on a new level of awareness because we had felt and known the presence of universal Love.

Here we see the principle of subjective dominion illustrated in a wonderful way. Having tried for some months to deal with the relationship problem as something between herself and her husband, this woman spontaneously "repented" of that which was calling itself *herself.* "I felt a great desire to put my misery behind me — all its selfishness, pride, and fear. It was not worth holding on to. Mentally I put it down, let go of the whole weight of it."

To "repent" means to "turn around" and go in the opposite direction. The release of the self and its contents of "selfishness, pride, and fear," freed consciousness immediately to be aware of universal Love, the substance of reality. But even more surprising, the release of her self sense released her husband's as well. He came up from the basement to be enveloped, like his wife, in the awareness of divine Love.

In the presence of that Soul sense, the ego problems simply never came up again. "The discords of a petty, limited sense of existence no longer claimed our attention. We were able to live on a new level of awareness because we had felt and known the presence of universal Love." How clearly this illustrates that ego values are self-seen and self-released in the light of Soul values. Even though we may not have such a wonderfully dramatic experience, the conscious, daily celebration of spiritual qualities gradually has the very same effect of refining our sense of what is good and of what belongs to our experience.

The practicality of bliss in ordinary family situations is shown in the following report from a "Mrs. D. E.":

> On one occasion I felt particularly helpless. It was not a dramatic situation by the usual standards. My two sons, aged ten and eight, were quarrelling in the adjacent room. It was a typically childish argument over a trifle, but I felt part of me rising up in annoyance and impatience. I was tired after a long day. My three-year-old daughter was sitting at the ta-

ble repeatedly refusing to eat her dinner. My husband, perhaps with some justification, not apparent to me at the time, gruffly demanded his customary but hitherto overlooked cup of tea! The boys began to endanger themselves with their fighting. In that instant I knew that the irritability of the lower half of my personality would explode into a disproportionately angry outburst. Even as I walked toward the boys with my hands raised ready to thrust them apart roughly, I cried out to my God in my heart. (I cannot describe my earnestness simply as prayer — it was very much a cry to God. It was actually word-less, a rapid thinking experience without the use of words — but I cannot convey that to paper.) As nearly as I can describe it my approach to God was, "Lord, I love them. I do not want to hurt them. Left to myself I am helpless. Help me, my God! I freely submit my will, my mind, everything that is in me — for their sakes!"

As I arrived at the spot where the boys stood, I found that it was not I who acted at all. I felt that some power other than myself controlled me, but it was a power of love which could be trusted. My hands were gentle as I separated the combat-ants — I could feel the love flowing out towards them — and they instantly clung one to each side of me, both smiling lov-ingly and happily up at me. In their eyes was a simple trust that I have never seen in them before or since....

I then turned to the baby and spoke to her. It was as if it were not I who determined what words were to be spoken. I do not even remember what they were. I do know, however, that my voice was gentle, and that the little one picked up her spoon and began to eat contentedly. I turned to my husband and found him quietly preparing the tea.

For the brief space of time here outlined, I was an entirely different personality. There was no "self" demanding atten-tion. It was as if all of me were outgoing. But more than that, the most vivid impression was that my will had disappeared.[25]

Here again the principle of dominion in consciousness proves itself. Releasing her own "self" and "will" in the conscious appeal to God and to divine Love, Mrs. D. E. finds that universal Love flooding the entire scene, releasing her whole family from the tyranny of self-centered feelings and friction.

To the personal level of thought, interpersonal power is essential. To give up one's "will" is to invite domination by others. It is only when we see that we can and actually do live in a universe of spiritual oneness that the release of the will that belongs to the belief of separate identity makes sense. Rather than leaving us helpless, the release of human will allows the whole field of our activity to be invaded by the harmony and benevolence of the spiritual universe.

CHAPTER 5

Soul-lutions to Ego Problems

The light of the body is the eye: if therefore thine eye be single, thy whole body shall be full of light. But if thine eye be evil, thy whole body shall be full of darkness.

— JESUS (MATTHEW 6:22–23)

Even if the sun were to rise from the west, the Bodhisattva has only one way. The Bodhisattva's way is called the "single-minded way" or "one railway track thousands of miles long."

— SHUNRYU SUZUKI[26]

Dominion versus Power

Okay, so the chapter title is a bit corny. But it gives us a mental picture of a crucial distinction. The difference between so-lutions and Soul-lutions is absolute, and we need to have it clear and fixed in our thinking. Soul identity is the ultimate solution to all the problems to which ego identity gives rise.

We need that corny word — "Soul-lutions" — to bounce up in front of our inner eyes again and again, because otherwise we'll keep getting hooked into some sort of power struggle all the time. Since persons see themselves separate from an external world to which they remain vulnerable in every way, the quest for power over that external world arises incessantly in human affairs. Power over some external person, place, or thing is perceived by the ego to be its only guarantee of safety and the primary means to getting the good for itself. That's why seeking solutions within consciousness may seem silly and futile to us, unless we are forearmed with that Soul-word.

Everything comes to us at the point of consciousness. We may think something is outside of us, but we deal with it only as we become conscious of it. And at that point, it is actually a mental picture, not an external thing, with which we are dealing. Just yesterday, this idea saved me from a big, ego-induced hassle. I had my kitchen repainted. After the painters left, I was certain that they had misplaced a light fixture, and I tried to get them to come back and locate it. The head painter said that there had been no fixture and got increasingly angry as I insisted that there had been. I was getting very upset about the "poor service" and fearful of the painter's anger as well, when suddenly my awareness shifted from the outer picture to my own thinking. I saw the sense of tension, the belief of hostile interaction. I felt the futility of pushing against an angry, defensive mentality, and I spontaneously "repented" of it. I thought, "It isn't worth it." I was willing to drop the issue for the sake of peace. Shortly thereafter, I realized what the painter had been telling me, and that he was correct. I felt very embarrassed, and I apologized to him. And I gave a great big "thank you very much" to Soul for once again saving my opinionated, self-righteous ego from its just deserts.

The ego has a very hard time dropping an issue about which it feels righteous. But the ego can be mistaken, as I was in this instance. Moreover, the ego is *always* mistaken in terms of the big picture. Something bigger and better is always taking place, and a desire to see the bigger picture is Soul's reminder to us of our real need. In a paraphrase of the First Commandment, Hora advises: "Thou shalt have no other interests before the good of God, which is spiritual." Because the good of God is spiritual, it is found in consciousness, or not at all.

The two quotations that begin this chapter both point to the subjective nature of life issues. The "single eye" is the Soul eye. The "Bodhisattva's single-minded way" is the way of seeing from the standpoint of oneness. In this chapter we will explore the effects of this way of seeing on human problems, beginning with relationship issues.

Marianne Williamson writes:

> When we're not in a relationship, the ego makes it seem as though all the pain would go away if we were. If the re-

lationship lasts, however, it will actually bring much of our existential pain to the surface. That's part of its purpose. It will demand all of our skills at compassion, acceptance, release, forgiveness, and selflessness....

Relationships don't necessarily take the pain away. The only thing that "takes the pain away" is a healing of the things that cause the pain.[27]

My mother used to say, "Marriage doesn't solve anything." That statement, I think, came out of her own disappointment with marriage, and for that I am sorry. But the statement is true, and I am glad to have known it. As plans for our marriage unfolded, Jan and I were told, "You are not the solution to each other's problems. But your marriage is the fruit of each of you resolving your problems."

One of the great gifts of our marriage has been that we have understood from the first that "marital problems" are not *marital* problems but *consciousness* problems, to be resolved in consciousness. Recently someone asked Jan for the secret to a long and harmonious marriage. He replied, "My approach has been to see every interpersonal problem as a personal problem that only I can resolve." And the key to this approach is noticing which "I" is doing our thinking and seeing.

Soul-Based Reasoning

When we appeal to "I," Soul, we automatically detoxify the mental climate, because we begin with spiritual facts rather than ego beliefs and feelings. Soul identity appears on the human level as understanding, and understanding yields a capacity to reason from intelligent, constructive, and nonpersonal ideas. Ego issues always involve personalities, feelings, and wants. The belief that one is a human personality with its own feelings and wants inevitably leads to friction with other personalities and their feelings and wants. And no real resolution is possible within that framework. At best, we can only negotiate compromises.

Soul identity looks to consider *values* instead of personalities, *issues* instead of feelings, and *needs* instead of wants. In long-term relation-

ships, there are many issues that must be discussed and resolved and
legitimate needs to be considered. Intelligence and love can resolve all
legitimate issues, as long as personal sense doesn't sabotage thinking
with its agenda of personal desires and feelings.

When a problem arises, then, the place to start is to take a look at
your own thinking. Ask yourself: "What is my problem here? What
is the personal belief that is declaring that there is a problem?" Then
see if you can separate the real issue from self-centered feelings and
desires. This is relatively easy when one's standard is joint participation
in quality living. Then our concern will be, "What is needed here for
family harmony, peace, and health?" rather than, "What do I want or
feel like doing?" or "What do I think he/she/they should be doing?"
By asking the right questions, the legitimate issues can be sorted out
from the clamor of ego claims.

Only when we consider interpersonal issues from a Soul-based standard can there be lasting solutions. This is so because it is only on a
universal level that the lawfulness of good that can provide a reliable
foundation is found. This requires, practically, being willing to question our personal feelings and desires, not in order to subserve another
person's feelings and desires, but in service to our own Soul identity
and Its agenda of spiritual unfoldment. As the young man we mentioned in the last chapter put it to his buddy, it's a question of what
kind of a man or woman we want to *be*.

Who says what's a problem and what isn't? Bliss reports are devoid
of any sense of problem. In bliss consciousness, there are no problems
because there is no self to experience problems. The message of bliss
is that a party is always going on in the Father's house to which we, as
His offspring, are invited. Bliss beckons us to remember who we are,
so that we may return home from the "far country" of self-existence.
Every time we turn from ego engagement with an external situation
and seek the comfort and guidance of Soul being, we find the Father
welcoming us to the party with open arms.

The Price of Personal Solutions

A recent story in the paper illustrates very graphically and poignantly
the importance of dealing with problems subjectively, on a Soul- rather

than an ego-basis. In a high school classroom, in front of the class, a sixteen-year-old boy shot himself in the head. He did it because he was distraught about his girlfriend breaking up with him. She was in the class, and he wanted her to see him kill himself so that she would blame herself. He had told the girl and others that if she refused to keep dating him he would do this, and he carried through his plan. The boy lived, without brain damage, but with much of his jaw and mouth blown away.

This is a personal solution to a personal problem, and not only is nothing solved, but, to human sense, great damage has been done. Self-confirmation was the initiator of action here, which shows how immoral and self-destructive the self's standards can be. The Soul betrayal in this action is so blatant that we can only stand aghast at the ego's capacity to hide its folly from itself. The need for a Soul standard from which to judge our thinking thus stands starkly revealed.

From the standpoint of Soul values, such an act could never have taken place. Love and intelligence are primary Soul values, aspects of God. Knowing that, we know without question that any thinking and behavior that are unloving and unintelligent will never work well. We know that when we are in emotional pain, the need is to get to a level of thought where Love and intelligence can heal the hurt rather than acting on the basis of the belief that creates the pain.

In Matthew 7:18–20, Jesus says,

> A good tree cannot bring forth evil fruit, neither can a corrupt tree bring forth good fruit. Every tree that bringeth not forth good fruit is hewn down, and cast into the fire. Wherefore by their fruits ye shall know them.

Having the capacity to judge our own beliefs by their fruits and to "hew down and cast into the fire" those beliefs that do not bear good fruit is one of the great gifts of Soul identity. Ego tends to become defensive when its agenda goes bankrupt and to look around for someone to blame. But if we can face up to the consequences of our actions and let the betraying beliefs surface and be released, we need not suffer their bankruptcy over and over.

The young man's actions proved that his girlfriend was right to reject him. A very good way to unmask ego operations is to look at the actions that it promotes in our thinking and then ask ourselves:

"Would doing this prove me to be loving and intelligent and therefore worthy of the other person's affection?" Asking this question would reduce the murders involving "estranged" lovers and wives that take place with such incredible regularity. The sheer malice expressed in trying to kill oneself in front of one's supposed "loved one" or to kill the loved one is staggering. Thus, object-oriented "love" is revealed to be essentially unloving and potentially destructive. It is a devil. And devils are no good!

Dominion over Devils

The first step in having dominion over devil beliefs is depersonalizing them so that they can be seen and evaluated as beliefs. People are not devils; mistaken beliefs are devils. And we are much more likely to be able to evaluate their fruits if they are seen as beliefs rather than as persons.

Second, our evaluation of beliefs must take place from some standard above the whole spectrum of ego-based beliefs if the essential devilishness is to be discerned and destroyed. One of the most troublesome aspects of thinking from the standpoint of personhood is that the concern tends to be with how our lives *look* rather than with the quality of them. Since personal experience is essentially dramatic, we think we're supposed to be the director of our own scenarios: "You, stand over there! You, get out of the picture...you're not in this shot. Bring in the happy kids. You, smile! You're having a great time."

When we can't get our experiences to look the way we think they should, we get anxious and frustrated. We blame others and ourselves and try to operate on those we blame to make them conform. Discord is increased rather than lessened by a judgmental and manipulative mentality. They and we resist being operated on like some mindless lump of clay. So then we become depressed and resentful. (At this moment half the people I know are either muttering under their breath that they wish they were dead, or are so angry at others that they would like to kill them. And these people are all to outward appearances living lives of great success and abundance. There isn't a Rwandan refugee in the lot!) Sometimes — much too often, as we have noted —

people resort to the grossest form of manipulation, that is, violence, and precipitate a tragedy.

Unless the underlying mistake gets corrected, the situation can only repeat and repeat, like a broken record. "The good that I would, I do not; but the evil which I would not, that I do," wailed St. Paul, recognizing that "in me [that is, in my flesh] dwelleth no good thing: for to will is present with me; but how to perform that which is good I find not" (Rom. 7:19, 18). This is the existential cry of a man who discerns the futility of attempting to find and live the good from the standpoint of material identity ("my flesh") in which is "no good thing." Out of such a discernment, we are ready to ascend out of the "old man" of personal identity into the "new man" of our Soulness.

The issue is not making our lives take a certain form and shape, because happiness does not lie in any form or shape. So others do not have power over our happiness, nor does it require a performance by ourselves of which we are incapable. *Happiness is the awareness of the quality substance of Life.* Actually, the only reason we set up the mental scenarios that we do and try to bring them about is that we think that we would feel happy if only our lives looked like that. But it works the other way around. Coming to feel a degree of contentment because we are seeing the already present good of God, we find our experiences shifting naturally to reflect more and more of that good.

Getting clear with ourselves that we are not here to stage our personal lives to our personal satisfaction chops through the root of our cycles of effort, frustration, and blame.

Polly Berends writes:

> Perhaps our parents did not fail us in the past, and we are not failing each other now! Maybe it has always only been some mistaken idea — a false expectation or ignorant assumption letting us down — a false *idea* of God letting down a false *idea* of self.... In every case it is an idea, a false expectation, that betrays us. It is never, at bottom, each other.[28]

When Jesus sent out seventy of his chosen disciples to prepare the people for his subsequent visits, they returned greatly impressed with the power that he had given them. "Our Lord, even the demons have submitted to us in your name," they declared "with great joy." After acknowledging the power given and the fact that because of it "nothing shall harm you," Jesus directed their attention to a higher issue: "But do not rejoice in this, that the demons submit to you; but rejoice because your names are written in heaven" (Luke 10:17, 20).

Dominion over demons is not a personal power but is incidental to the realization of one's Soul name, "written in heaven" for all eternity. As Soul values change our definition of the good, attachments to limited, personal "goods" are brought to the surface. This may be experienced as demons or problems — emotional, relational, situational, and physical — but they surface in the process of being displaced by a new, higher sense of ourselves. As we "rejoice that our names are written in heaven," the belief of names written on earth, together with their values and the problems they invite, lessen.

Angels Within

It was recently reported that nearly 70 percent of the American people believe in angels. Most of these believe in a personal guardian angel, which keeps watch over them. I love the idea of angels. Psalm 91 assures us that "He shall give his angels charge over thee, to keep thee in all thy ways." I think that the idea of a guardian angel is one of the most meaningful ways in which our Soul name takes form for us, while we still think of ourselves as persons.

Angels are benevolent, divine Life in an external form and shape. One's Soul name is the same benevolent, divine Life, experienced within rather than externally. Our Soul name is our inner angel, protecting and guiding us from within consciousness. The sense of divine Presence is the important thing, whether we call it an angel or Soul name. But the more we locate the benevolence within, the more certain it becomes and the more it operates to dissolve the beliefs about ourselves that are the source and location of our problems. When we understand that angels are *subjective*, not objective, then we are not only blessed by their presence, but our own identity is seen as angelic rather than demonic. Angels within displace and dissolve devils within.

Problems as Pointers

Having clarified that personal ego beliefs are devils, we can understand how "bad things happen to good people." The personal goodness of one's human identity does not protect that person from the beliefs that belong to that character's story. To be protected from harm, it is not enough to consider ourselves innocent persons. We must realize that our true identity is innocent *of personhood* in the same way that upon waking we find ourselves innocent of the events and actions that took place in the dream. Personhood is a target for problems, because ego sees itself as a target of negative, external forces. As persons, we are never out of range of potential problems.

From Soul's perspective, problems become pointers to something wonderful about Life that we have not yet discovered. The experience of lack points to an increasing discovery of abundance; illness points us to see more of the wholeness of Life; fear points us to the discovery of Love; and so on. This helps us refrain from automatically hating and trying to get rid of problems. They can bring to our attention aspects of ego identity that operate to obscure Soul awareness.

This was the case with a woman I spoke with some years ago. She was desperately trying to conceive a baby and had failed to do so, even though doctors found her and her husband in perfect physical condition. She had tried everything medically and spiritually that she knew to do, and the seeming barrenness continued. "All of my life, since I was five years old," she said, "I have known that the only thing I ever wanted was to be a mother. And now my time is running out, and I can't stand the pain of not having a child."

This woman grew up in a very dysfunctional family in which she received very little mothering from her mother. Clearly, her desire for a baby was a desire to "get" a mother by being a mother and "be" a baby by having a baby. And that's okay. That's the joy of parenthood for everyone: we get to redo our childhood at the same time as enjoying parenthood. But the insistence that she must have a baby was one of those ego demands on Life to look a certain way that, I felt, was covering up some underlying issues.

In later sessions, the woman began to talk about a lifelong sense of adversarialness of which motherhood had become the focus. She said, "I have always had an adversarial sense toward God, that I had to 'duke it out' with God to get the things I want in my life." And she confessed that as an attorney being a tough litigator had been her ideal. It was pointed out that just getting a baby into her house wouldn't heal that embattled sense and might, indeed, heighten it. Many mothers come to feel, at times, that their baby is their adversary. She was encouraged to "Spirit feast" daily, looking for and loving to see all the present evidences of good in her experience.

As the woman began to pay attention to the bounty and beauty of her real Life, she began to notice that her professional ideal was shifting to attorney as adviser rather than as litigator. She was more drawn to be supportive and instructive of clients than to "go to war" on their behalf. She also realized that she had been thinking that having a baby would automatically release her deprived, embattled sense of herself. She recognized that that sense needed to be healed first, so that she would be able to conceive of herself as loving mother/ loved child. Then the physical conception that reflected that mental conception could take place.

Spiritual Innocence from Origin-al Sin

Soul identity is the source of solutions to ego problems because our innocence of personhood renders us innocent of origin-al sin, that is, the false belief of having a human origin. In Soul, we claim our total freedom from the belief of life apart from God. Once when I was feeling very impeded in my life by another person, I was told, "The mistake is not that another can impede, but that you have any life or capacity of your own, apart from the divine, that can be impeded." The solution is not to see another person differently or see an external situation differently, but to see *oneself* differently. Either the divine Life and Mind are our Life and Mind here and now, or we have no life and no mind. But we do not have the option of having little, material lives and little, personal minds. That's a belief, a misconception that we neither created nor chose. So we do not have to settle for it.

Several years ago I ran across a comment by Jacob Needleman to the effect that our society suffers from "metaphysical repression." In the same way that sexuality was kept under wraps in Victorian times, conscious awareness and open discussion of transpersonal issues has been kept out of sight in our culture. This is yielding considerably at the present time. But we are still, I think, largely misguided and even tyrannized by the beliefs and values that are culturally dominant. We still tend to judge ourselves by comparison with people who appear successful according to cultural values: money, fame, power, sexual attraction, personal achievement.

In the light of spiritual values, however, we may find a sense of regret arising for the years of Soul betrayal rather than for failing to fit in with others' ego agendas. A man who was raised in a very rigid, punitive environment found himself wracked with uncontrollable sobs for much of a day. He kept repeating, "I'm sorry, I'm so sorry," without any idea of what the apology meant. The episode followed his having discovered a photo of himself at age two. In the photo he was wearing a very gaudy pair of sunglasses and had a big, impish grin on his face.

Looking at that photo, the man had felt outraged to see himself "humiliated, wearing such dopey, gaudy girl's sunglasses." He said, "I wonder who put those on me." I said, "Maybe that little guy put them on himself. I'll bet he didn't think they were stupid or gaudy and didn't feel humiliated. I'll bet he thought they were the hottest things around. But notice your reaction, and see what it tells you about what happened to that innocent, playful little imp."

I think this man's gut-wrenching sobs of apology are his first appreciative acknowledgement of his innocence and spontaneity, so long kept locked away from even his own awareness. He was not to blame for the threatening environment that required the repression of so many of his positive qualities. Even so, there is often a sense of ego conspiracy against our own best selves as long-repressed qualities come to light. I have cried many tears of regret myself as the inherent Soul betrayal of egoAnn identity has come to light.

As the child aspects of this man's Soul identity are released, he will find as well his loving fatherness emerging. Ultimately, no apology will be necessary, since all blame will be seen as irrelevant. Montague glimpsed the truth that saves us: "What if here we are only symbols of ourselves, and our real being is somewhere else, — perhaps in the heart of God?" Safe in the heart of God, "hid with Christ in God...." There...here...Soul identity, in all its inviolate holiness, awaits our discovery.

Anger and Justice

One of the most captivating issues to the ego is the belief that life should be fair and isn't. Anger is chronic and endemic on the human level because personal existence proves itself unlawful and unjust again and again. Yet we retain a deep sense that life should be fair. The mistake we make is thinking that it should be fair *according to our personal terms and definitions of fairness*. Years ago I learned the folly of this concept of justice from observing one of my sons when he was three years old. As is often the case at that age, he was working hard to get the rules straight. Recalling the incident in the course of preparing a paper on anger and justice, I wrote:

> I asked him, politely, to pick up his toys. I said "Please." Later, seeing them untouched, I repeated my polite request. I said, "Please pick up your toys right now and put them away." Later, seeing the toys still untouched, I became angry. No longer polite. I didn't say, "Please." I said, "Pick up your toys right now!" He looked up at me in shock and burst into tears. "You didn't say 'please,'" he cried. I tried to reason: "I said 'please' twice and it didn't do any good. So now I am not going to say 'please' anymore. Just pick up the toys."
>
> "No, no, no, no," he wailed. "You've gotta say 'please.'" And I watched, dumbfounded, as he got completely lost in the insistence. I offered him everything. I laughed, I apologized for my anger, I forgave him, I offered a reconciling hug — but nothing would do except "please." He was simply inconsolable.
>
> I saw in this little boy's misery an existential issue. I saw in that little self Everyself, hooked on its own terms, its own demands, its own very primitive, fragmented, and distorted sense of how life is supposed to be. And I saw how that insistence blinds us all, as it blinded him, to everything else. The whole human race, the human mind, is stuck, wailing, "No, no, no, no. You've gotta say 'please...'" or whatever it is that it thinks should be. "You gotta do this...you gotta not do that...you gotta!" And Life — or whoever represents Life to us at that moment — doesn't "gotta..." and won't. And so we are angry.[29]

There is no solution to our sense of injustice within the pages of our personal story. The only solution is a Soul-lution. Jesus could say, "Love your enemies, bless anyone who curses you, do good to anyone who hates you, and pray for those who carry you away by force and persecute you" (Matt. 5:44, Lamsa translation), not because he was totally bonkers, but because he spoke from Soul rather than ego.

Life is not experiences. Life is God. And God is not fair; God is the universal Principle of Love. "Even if the sun should rise from the west, the Bodhisattva [the enlightened individual] has only one way." It is to turn in thought to the one "I" and acknowledge no other law than Love and no other identity than Soul.

Soul's "Intercession"

Declaring our innocence of personhood can bless others in seemingly miraculous ways. When my mother was in the hospital during her final illness, she was put onto a respirator without my permission. She was ninety-two and desperately hoped to pass on, reminding us that my dad had termed pneumonia "the old people's friend," because it so often provides the "exit door." But the young, zealous doctor took heroic actions, and Mother ended up tied down hand and foot and head, with a tube stuffed down her throat, unable not only to move, but even to cry. I found the sight unbearable. Standing by her bedside, seeing the beseeching look in her eyes, I completely understood the feelings of a man I had read about who had forced a nurse at gunpoint to release his dying father from a respirator. On the way out, I expressed my anguish to the compassionate male nurse who was on duty, and he commented, "I understand how you feel. I would never let them do that to me."

Returning home, I realized that I couldn't just sit in my human thoughts and feelings about the situation. It was unbearable, and I knew that my emotional torture couldn't help relieve my mother's suffering. So I set myself to re-see the situation through Soul eyes rather than ego eyes. Soul sees only universal, spiritual realities. I acknowledged that the ICU was filled with all the love, intelligence, harmony, beauty, peace, and good of the divine universe. Each time the picture of an old woman being tortured by misguided medical technology arose, I saw it as *my temptation* rather than *her situation*. Refusing the temptation to let ego misrepresent the truth of spiritual good, I exercised my Soul-based dominion in consciousness. As long as I didn't let thought be drawn out into a seeming external situation, within which both she and I were helpless, I found that the horror and panic diminished. I felt an increasing sense of assurance in my capacity to celebrate God's presence and power as the only reality, no matter what the human viewpoint was claiming.

I deliberately stayed away from my mother's bedside until the next day, even though humanly I felt guilty about it. I knew that she would be most greatly blessed if I could get absolute clarity about the truth of being before I returned. When I saw her the next day, I had been talking with her for five minutes before I noticed that the respirator tube was out. (This, to me, indicated how completely the picture had been dissolved in my own thinking.) When I expressed gratitude to the nurse on the way out, he said, "We didn't take the tube out; it fell out. I've never seen anything like it!" I left the hospital that day in a thrill of gratitude. And that grand evidence of the power and presence of Love continues to bless my thought.

Re-Souling the Past

The stuff of ego identity is the past. The standard by which the ego judges everything is that of what has been. It evaluates everything that comes up in the light of what it knows from the past and that past seems fixed, for good or for ill. When we think from a consciousness standpoint, however, we make a wonderful discovery: the past isn't past, at all. It has no objective existence "back there." It is a present mental picture that, like all pictures presenting themselves to us at the point of consciousness, can be directly addressed right here, right now.

Re-souling the past is, then, no different from dealing in consciousness with any current issue that presents itself. The basic principle is that instead of trying to operate on an external situation we look at the mental picture with Soul eyes, which see, as real and present, the universal, eternal qualities of the divine Life. It may be even easier to re-see the past than to see through some of the pictures that call themselves "the present."

All of us have particular vignettes from our own childhood that come to mind repeatedly. These represent moments of particular self-awareness, even if the situation was not of great significance. They are remembered because they picture our basic sense of ourselves as persons. It is useful to take these pictures and re-see the situation in light of our present understanding of spiritual reality. As children we saw through extremely narrow lenses and had no way to think about our situation in larger terms. Now we can add the divine dimension to the picture.

For example, one woman remembered sitting in a chair watching a Winnie the Pooh cartoon on TV when she was about six years old. She heard her brother and father arguing in the next room. Her parents were divorced, and she and her brother lived with their father. She remembers an acute sense of sadness, especially in contrast to the charming story on TV. She felt intensely the discrepancy between her feelings of discord and loss and "how little kids are supposed to feel" as represented by Winnie the Pooh.

As an adult, she practiced re-seeing that situation from a Soul viewpoint: seeing the whole room filled with divine Love. She saw the TV program as being evidence to her, in a form appreciable to a six-year-old, of the essential goodness of life, which was true despite the argument between her father and brother. She acknowledged, "Never has there been a moment in God's kingdom where a single quality of good has been missing. Love doesn't know a sad or lonely child. That room was filled with Love, even if the human child couldn't see it at that time." As she practiced this kind of re-vision of her memory, she became increasingly aware that she was greatly blessed to have her father, a very caring man, take custody of her and her brother; that her mother, despite her problems, loved them as much as she could; and that throughout her childhood every need was met and she was surrounded by support and benevolence. She saw that this was true, despite her little girl's ego sense of sad loneliness. This helped her find release from the chronic depression, based upon that deprived-child picture that had continued to cloud her consciousness.

Resolving Parent-Child Issues

As persons, nothing is more important and lasting than parental influence. Our human identity sense is largely determined by the way our parents saw themselves, which was a product of how their parents saw themselves, and on and on into the past. Many people feel conscious frustration and even rage at being so limited and determined by parental thinking. Personal identity has nothing to offer in terms of getting beyond parental influence. It tries to escape by putting spacial or emotional distance between itself and its parents. But the very drive to keep away confirms the power of the influence, and even a parent's death doesn't resolve the issues.

The only real transcendence of any human issue lies in finding a different identity, one whose source is not human but is divine. "Call no man your father upon the earth," said Jesus, "for one is your Father, which is in heaven" (Matt. 23:9). The same goes for "mother." Yet the Ten Commandments instruct us to honor our earthly parents. The two injunctions actually complement each other, for it is only by seeing our human parents in their divine identity that we can truly honor them. And it is only as we are able to honor their true being that we can fully realize our own. We cannot feel embraced by Soul identity as long as human identity remains fixed by grudges, debts, desires, or guilt toward our human parents.

One of the primary psychological factors in relation to our parents is that we continue to see them from an infantile perspective in which they assume godlike proportions. This leads us to think that their behavior toward us was intentional and that they could have behaved differently — and certainly would have if they had loved us properly! Coming to see our parents as just people, like us, who did the best they could within their ego beliefs, constitutes a big step along the way to releasing the spell of parental influence.

Some years ago the following letter was passed on to me. I believe it comes from an EST newsletter, but I have no other information about it. The writer tells how each year he visits his parents, hoping to make the visit be "perfect." Yet each time he ends up in a hassle with his mother and leaves feeling like a failure. On his last visit, however, something different happened. When he found himself arguing with his mother and his stomach sank with despair, he suddenly "woke up."

I found myself looking across the table at an altogether very nice sixty-five-year-old woman. For a moment, I also saw myself. I saw that, as two individuals, each of us is very much in the process of working through the issues of our lives. I saw that being mother and son doesn't change the facts of who we are, or of what we have to learn. Having the relationship that we do merely provides the special opportunity of going through this learning process together.

Somehow, at that moment, the entire context of our relationship changed for me. I could no longer feel guilty or inadequate about the fact that each of us is just the way we are. I could only feel grateful for it.... It was no longer necessary to have anything be different, to have the circumstances of each interaction be "perfect." It was already perfect!

At about this time in our visit, I began to view my mother as the *perfect teacher* — one whose purpose it has been to keep revealing my childish patterns of reaction until I finally let go of them....

The remainder of my visit was somehow different. I continued to regard my mother as the perfect teacher, and when there were conflicts in our interactions, I merely observed them.... In the several days that remained, I actually saw myself growing up by leaps and bounds — letting go of lifelong resentments and reactive patterns which have only served to keep me small....

As the trip drew to a close, we parted knowing our mutual love, loyalty and support as the fundamental truth of our relationship.... There is no longer the sense that anything has to be any different, or more perfect. It already is.[30]

The heart of the writer's insight is that "it was no longer necessary ... to have the circumstances of each interaction be 'perfect.' It was already perfect!" The spiritual universe is already perfect. *The significance of human interactions lies in the degree to which we can use them to see through the misconceptions of human life rather than the degree to which they satisfy those misconceptions.* Seeing himself and his mother as joint participants in that consciousness process, the writer is able to use the relationship for his own spiritual growth rather than trying to manage it for ego comfort, an enterprise that had continually gone bankrupt and left him with "a sense of incompletion and failure."

James Redfield suggests that we find our special lifetime quest by understanding what each of our parents valued and stood for and then "discovering a truth that is a higher synthesis of what these two believed."[31] This is a different task from that of discovering the negative, limiting aspects of parental beliefs and behavior. It is a recognition that we are not condemned simply to act out the personal and interpersonal patterns of our family mentality but have an existential destiny to find and express the best values of both sides of our human heritage.

I like this positive take on parental determinations. It is the fact of Soul, the fact that we are ultimately not persons at all, that gives rise to the impulse to transcend the straightjacket of personal identity and to "honor [our] father and our mother" by more fully expressing the best qualities and values of both.

Although self-sacrifice and a consequent sense of personal demand and lack belonged to my mother's personal identity, that's not what her life was *about*. Her Soul identity was very much in evidence in her eye for beauty and her great interest in and love for people.

My father was a pediatrician, the first in the state of Idaho. He and my mother married, not for romance, although they were deeply fond and appreciative of each other, but in order to share a work of helping and healing children and their families. My mother's background as a psychiatric social worker specializing in child welfare fit well with Dad's medical practice. Dad was a wonderful, creative doctor, who was devoted to "his" babies.

However, he was not a very good father. Emotionally he was very immature and required Mother's total support in every aspect of his life and work. My brother, I think, was regarded by Dad largely as a rival for my mother's attention, and he always felt he could do nothing right in Dad's eyes. My father doted on me, but it was a blind affection that didn't seem to touch me because he didn't see me in my own right at all. He was fifty-two when I was born, and as a teenager I hated him for being old and funny-looking and hated myself more for hating him.

But as I have been concerned to release my personal identity for the sake of Soul awareness, my negative feelings toward my father have dropped away in an increasing appreciation for his sweetness, fidelity, intelligence, and kindness. The love of children, the devotion to serving the health and well-being of entire families, and the creativity and intuitiveness of his professional judgments were what his life was *about.*

Personal identity is shaped and formed by our human parents' beliefs. What Soul does is rescue the positive qualities of our parents from the limitations and negativity of their ego stuff so that we are blessed by their highest values and aspirations while releasing, increasingly, the negative aspects of their and our ego beliefs.

Our Parents' Soul Identity

Our parents were or are here to work out their salvation with God. We cannot do that for them. The truth of their being is already Soul, and it is to the care of their own Soul identity that we commit them in our prayers even while being humanly supportive. My mother, whom we invited to live with us when she was eighty-two, was unable even to think about, let alone discuss with me, her fears about her situation. She wanted things from me that I couldn't give and unwittingly rejected the things I did have to give, which could have helped her. She wanted me to solve her problems for her, to keep her from having to go to a nursing home, her dread of which became a self-fulfilling prophecy. The day we placed her in a nursing home was the worst day of my life, and perhaps of hers.

But Jan helped me see that I couldn't save her from the consequences of her own ego beliefs, and that Life didn't require me to go down trying. Throughout that day and the days that followed my grief and guilt were frequently interrupted by the thought, "But doesn't God still love her?" This brought me out of the cloud of ego preoccupation and back to a grateful acknowledgment that God remains God, however important little persons may fancy themselves to be. And God's universe of good is always the truth of every situation.

Mother actually improved, physically and mentally, in the nursing home, where she made friends. She was a trooper all her life and met that challenge with the same quiet fortitude that so characterized her. I don't think she ever made sense of her situation though. It took me some years after her passing to fully release the ego claims of guilt, sadness, and regret. But I knew the toxic nature of guilt and blame and never believed that indulging in those feelings could do her any more good than it could do me.

My concern has been to release us both into the light of Soul, that universal quality awareness that is the true home and identity of us both. One of the fruits of this focus was the writing of a book about motherhood.[32] As the book was completed I felt that it was a fulfillment for my mother as well as for me. The mother qualities that so shone through Mary, despite her personal beliefs, were expressed through the book in a way that honored her more than any personal recognition could. Actually, I now see that it expressed my father's best qualities and highest values as well. In this way does Soul heal the seeming hurts and needs of the past and fulfill our parents' best intentions, blessing us all in the process.

> The Lord hath appointed me ... to give unto them that mourn ... beauty for ashes, the oil of joy for mourning, the garment of praise for the spirit of heaviness; that they might be called trees of righteousness, the planting of the Lord, that he might be glorified. (Isa. 61:1, 3)

Soul Seeing Reports

The following report is by a Zen student at the time of enlightenment. She writes:

> An enormous happiness came over me ... [and a] sense of gratitude that began flowing so strongly that it was very nearly beyond bearing. ...
>
> Such extraordinary happiness makes you realize ... how truly unhappy you had been before. Not in the life circumstances but in your *self*, your miserable, restless, eternally dissatisfied self. This joy is the joy of dropping burdens, burdens you didn't even know you had — so deeply had they entered you — dragging you down ... making you weigh heavy as lead, move as sluggishly as thick, cold molasses. ...

The writer's graphic depiction of how ego sense operates in consciousness to darken, disturb, and weigh us down makes it easier to spot the real culprit. Then we are not so apt to get involved in trying to fix what *it* says is wrong and are better able to dismiss the whole sense itself. The writer continues:

The lines written by a Christian mystic appeared in my head:

> All shall be well
> and all shall be well
> and all manner of things
> shall be well...

Yes! I thought. And not only *shall* all be well, all is well *right now!* And always had been well, only I had been too blind to see it. The incredible combination of fortunate circumstances that had led me to this moment, including all those I had considered blackest misfortune... all formed an intricate and loving pattern leading me... to this moment, preventing a headlong impetuosity that this middle-aged frame could not have supported, teaching me patience, feeding me disappointments and humiliations at a pace I could absorb, carrying me forward exactly in the right way, for me. And I knew the same miracles were unfolding for everyone....

I became aware that the pain of longing was completely gone. For what did I lack?[33]

Even without a bliss experience such as this, we often recognize in retrospect that what we had considered a terrible event, such as a divorce or job loss, turned out to be "the best thing that could have happened." Ego could never recognize a need for "disappointments and humiliations," yet as aspects of the bankruptcy of ego beliefs, they are inevitable and even important. But, as the writer indicates, at the initiative of Soul in the process of enlightenment these things come in just the right way for us. In moments of Soul awareness, everything in our experience falls into positive place as making a contribution to the Soul seeing that is heaven itself. Only gratitude is then felt, for nothing personal sense offers could ever compete with the bliss of seeing Life in its spiritual wholeness.

The following incident, reported by her sister, occurred to Doris Henty, an English woman who devoted her life to the practice of Christian Science healing. As a girl Doris had suffered from "carious bones in her face and head" for which she had had many operations and which doctors predicted would soon kill her. Along with other members of her family, she was healed when her mother read *Science and Health* by Mary Baker Eddy. Although the disease was arrested and feeling was restored to her face, Doris still suffered from distorted features where the bone had dissolved. Her sister reports:

> Then, one day, she read in a local paper that a cousin had won a beauty competition. Rather sadly she said, "I could never do that," but then she added, "But I have the beauty of holiness." She went to her schoolroom and all morning she thought about the beauty of holiness. At lunchtime, when she came down, Mother exclaimed, "Doll, have you seen your face?" Doris replied, "God cannot see a mortal face: He can only see the beauty of holiness." By the evening, her whole face had moved round to a normal angle.[34]

This is a wonderfully revealing report, because it enables us to see how this remarkable transformation of Doris's appearance took place. Her first response to the announcement in the paper that her cousin had won a beauty contest is a personal one: "Oh, I could never do that." Personally, her face is not beautiful, and she feels sad, excluded from the good and, perhaps, envious of her cousin. That's how things look through ego eyes.

But immediately there is a shift to the Soul viewpoint that brings immediate relief: "But I have the beauty of holiness." From have-not to have in a few seconds! The shift having taken place, her consciousness is then totally captivated with the view from the Soul window. She goes off to contemplate this wondrous fact of being, the beauty of holiness (wholeness) that is universal and ever untouched. When she comes down for lunch, her mother notices a change in her face and exclaims about it.

It is significant that Doris does not at this point say excitedly, "What? Has something happened to my face? Where's a mirror?" This would be the natural personal reaction to her mother's exclamation. But she is so totally fixed on the Soul level that she replies instead: "God cannot see a mortal face...." Here's a crucial point. Doris's consciousness dwelt for a whole day on a level of reality that was, and ever is, totally oblivious to material shapes and forms. God, the divine Mind and Life, does not know and does not live physical reality. The physical realm exists within a material misconception of what is actually and always a spiritual reality. The spiritual supersedes the material because the spiritual is what is actually *being*, everywhere, all the time. The material shapes and forms reflect the degree to which that spiritual substance is clear in consciousness.

Hence, when Doris comes down in the evening, after having spent the rest of the day being conscious of the beauty of holiness, her face has shifted. It better reflects the beauty of the wholeness of reality. Such a shift in picture is the incidental, though inevitable, consequence of dwelling in Soul awareness rather than personal sense. To Doris identity, there had been a memory of past illness, though healed. To Soul identity, there had never been anything to deface quality Life. As personal sense faded out in the awareness of Soul, so did the marks of that human memory.

The following statement summarizes the mental activity, based upon Soul identity, that alone offers real solutions to the problems of ego identity:

Today we let no ego thoughts direct our words or actions. When such thoughts occur, we quietly step back and look at them, and then we let them go. We do not want what they would bring with them. And so we do not choose to keep them. They are silent now. And in the stillness, hallowed by His Love, God speaks to us and tells us our will, as we have chosen to remember Him.

—A COURSE IN MIRACLES, LESSON 254

CHAPTER 6

Soul Activity

❧

Except the Lord build the house, they labour in vain that build it.
—PSALM 127:1

And seek not ye what ye shall eat, or what ye shall drink, neither
be ye of doubtful mind. For...your Father knoweth that ye have
need of these things. But rather seek ye the kingdom of God;
and all these things shall be added unto you. Fear not, little flock;
for it is your Father's good pleasure to give you the kingdom.
—LUKE 12:29–32

"Do I hafta do what I wanna do again today?" reportedly whined the
young student of a progressive school. I heard that story many years
ago, and it struck a chord with me. When I was single and living alone,
I often found it difficult to know what to do with myself, and I longed
for a structure that would dictate my activity. On the other hand, I
was also terrified of marriage and family for the very reason that it
would seemingly dictate my activity every moment of every day for all
time. With regard to activity, as to other aspects of a seemingly self-
and-others world, it often appears as if we are "damned if we do and
damned if we don't."

As children we seem to have very little freedom of choice in activity.
Adults largely decide what, where, when, and even how we will do
things. One big goal of teenagers is to become independent of adult
dictates regarding activity. But usually this is thought of in reactive
terms: "I want to do what *I* want, not what *they* want." Only when we
become adults do we realize that it is not at all easy to know what we
want to do, and often even harder to do it.

Work and Play

Personal identity thinks that activity is something that it must figure out and decide upon and then make happen. Ordinarily, for adults activity is divided into the primary categories of "work" and "play." Work is what we have to do and play is what we want to do. This "have to" versus "want to" frame of thought interrupts and corrupts our thinking about activity on the job and at home. Relationships with bosses and co-workers as well as with roommates or spouses suffer from the fallout from ego beliefs about activity. Many marriages founder upon issues of who does what, where, and when, both inside and outside the home.

The need to make money is the primary source of the sense of external requirement in adulthood, replacing the parental authority of childhood. I recently noticed that as long as making money is the primary motive for one's thinking about work, the job scene will tend to evoke and replay childhood feelings and thinking. One man, for example, has only to think of a structured job and he feels frantic and rebellious — just like he felt when as a young teenager he was sent to a juvenile detention center. Similarly, a woman raised in a totally restrictive and repressive home can envision herself only in a bottom-rung job totally determined by her superiors.

We run into trouble as egos even when we try to consider what we'd like to do. Putting the onus for fulfilling activity on personal ego, we may get the whole thing wrong. A man whose talents have gone virtually unexpressed and unfulfilled over six decades had told a friend who had suggested years before that he get counseling help: "I don't need help. I know how to make my dreams come true." Unfortunately he didn't realize that his ego's dreams were based upon its beliefs of lack and inadequacy, and those beliefs turned out to be the part of the dream that came true.

The Activity of the Whole

The only activity there is is the omniactivity of divine, quality Life. "Omni" means all, everywhere, so it is evident that if God is omniactive, then there can't also be separate, human activity going on in the same location. A moment's reflection enables us to see that we don't create ourselves or any of the capacities that we call "ours." Each morning we find ourselves conscious, awake, alive, with vitality, strength, and intelligence taking various forms through and as us. Our personal beliefs about ourselves shape the form of the activity to some degree, but that which is conscious and active is not personal beliefs but Mind and Life. Divine identity, Soul, is the source of the activity, not personal belief or fantasy.

Again we find ourselves in consciousness. Soul activity is mental, not physical, activity. Consciousness is the location and substance of spiritual activity and the only place where activity issues and problems can usefully be addressed. As before, the place to start is by taking a look at our usual ways of thinking about activity.

Professor David Bohm, a noted British physicist, found his studies carrying him into profound insights about consciousness. In a dialogue with Renee Weber, he commented,

> Everybody has some unique potential... a range of potentials. ... [But] the energy doesn't come from your predispositions. They must serve the whole. The energy comes from the whole...
>
> The individual *is* universal and the universal *is* the individual. The word "individual" means "undivided," so we could say that very few individuals have ever existed. We could call [most people] *dividuals.* Individuality is only possible if it unfolds from wholeness. Ego-centeredness is not individuality at all. Ego-centeredness is centered on the self-image which is an illusion and a delusion. Therefore it's nothing at all. True individuality means you have a true being which unfolds from the whole in its particular way for that particular moment.[35]

Ego tries to figure out what it wants to do by researching its "predispositions" — the particular beliefs of lack, limitation, and location that make up its sense of itself. It sees itself as the center of the issue and, as Bohm clarifies, this results in trying to figure out what we should do on the basis of "an illusion and a delusion." Ego doesn't do a very good job of informing us of the "range of potentials" that are available to us, since it is a *deficiency* lens, not an *efficiency* lens. Moreover, its belief of personal autonomy makes us feel like we must personally come up with the energy to get the activity done.

But all energy is universal energy, unlimited and unlocated. When we understand that Soul activity is in consciousness, then our priorities about activity shift, and we value above all time and place to realize ever afresh the omnipresence of quality Life. From this consciousness source flows the energy of the whole. As Soul identity dissolves the "illusion and delusion" of ego identity, we discover potential that we never dreamed could be ours. We find activity taking forms that we could never have considered or valued personally.

Trailblazing

Currently, the central activity of most of my days is a walk in what I call "the back country." This is a local flood plain behind a small dam, bordering a county park. It is criss-crossed with dirt roads and horse trails that must be reforged nearly every year after the winter-rain-produced streams and ponds have dried up and the lake has receded. It is real wilderness, the habitation of coyotes, bobcats, deer, snakes, rabbits, and an occasional mountain lion. Located in the middle of a huge urban area, its trails are traversed by a relatively few horse and bicycle riders, people walking large dogs, and hikers like myself.

Although we had visited the park many times over many years while our boys were growing up, I had never ventured outside the cultivated area. I saw trails leading off into the willows but couldn't imagine why anyone would want to follow them. I had begun taking a daily walk some years ago but kept to paved paths, even when the park was crowded and I longed for solitude.

Then my husband acquired a huge dog, a black Lab/pit bull combination, which he named Apollo. Apollo proved to be somewhat less than totally obedient, despite extensive and expensive training, and he needed space where he could run free. Jan began walking him out into the back country, and I followed along. Soon I was walking alone and enjoying the discovery of new trails. At first I was quite timid, and more than once I started along a trail into a willow woods only to turn back for fear of the unknown. But familiarity bred boldness, and my fear gave way to the thrill of exploration.

During the period of developing quality awareness, which followed the Denver trip described in chapter 2, I found that the back country walks took on an increasingly blissful dimension. The sense of the wholeness and fullness of life as manifested in the profusion of plants that grew up, jumbled together in an ocean of green and blossom, became intense. I had only to walk into the uncultivated fringe of the park to become immersed to some degree in a sense of the ravishing, ecstatic, mad beauty and unspeakable value of quality Life. Personal sense diminished substantially as I felt taken up into the wholeness of the scene.

Although the intensity of the bliss sense has faded generally and varies according to the degree of ego fog on any given day, these back-country walks continue to provide the best setting for daily consciousness-clearing. This walk is a daily pilgrimage to a green cathedral of wilderness that engulfs me in its holiness. On many occasions, as my gaze scans the multi-hued panorama of woods and hills and sky, the thought comes to mind: "This is My body, which is whole for you." Whole — whether dry or moist, brown or green, decaying or blooming — it is a wholeness of absolute beauty.

There is increasing interest in the idea of travel as pilgrimage. Many people find that taking a break from their ordinary activities to travel to locations of particular spiritual import elevates and refreshes consciousness in a way that benefits them greatly. I have found that these daily excursions into the wilderness qualify as pilgrimages, undertaken for the refreshment and renewal of my Soul sense. A friend who asked to be taken on a walk along the trails was amazed to hear me say that I more and more feel that this time in the back country is the most important activity of my day. "Most people would think that such activity is totally mundane and even a waste of time," she said. "After all, you don't really get anything done!"

For me, that is the importance of it. For one hour a day, my performer mode of thought is deactivated. In the midst of nature's continually shifting yet always beautiful abundance, it is easy to see that the good is given, is here. It is mine to enjoy as I am able to enjoy it. I "get" it just by seeing it, and in the seeing, I feel included in it. There, as nowhere else, I realize that "there is nothing to do. Just to be is a supremely total act." I feel free to venture and roam and play, without a single "have-to" or "should-have" on the horizon. Inevitably, that sense of transcendence blesses my doing-work the rest of the day. My counseling, writing, house and yard work, and shopping unfold with less effort and stress. And my husband, I am sure, finds me easier to live with.

But what I am increasingly understanding is that that hour is not just something that enables my human activity to proceed more effectively. It *informs* my busyness in a way that is leading me to call the whole ego context of activity into question. Ego living may be an everlasting, upward climb toward some sort of achievement. But Soul living is perennial pilgrimage, being about the business of witnessing to quality Life.

Soul Activity Is Art

Some months ago, listening to the radio, I heard a man touted as "the world's greatest living cellist" playing his cello. I thought about what a contribution such music makes to the world and about how this man's devotion to music must have consumed his thinking and activity for his entire life. Devoting himself completely to music, he became a channel for one of the most uplifting and healing forms of Soul available in human experience. This suggests to me that art is Soul activity. It follows that in Soul we are all artists, expressing the goodness that floods consciousness from a Soul standpoint.

The idea that Soul makes us artists of life is bringing a fresh angle on everything that I do. I notice that it is not all that easy to shift from reactive living to expressive living. Ego identity usually grounds itself in the very demands and threats that it so fears and hates. We know who and where we are by the familiar landmarks of what we have to do and what we are afraid of and whom we like and dislike. As I turn thought to a contemplation of the good, I often find myself, a moment later, locked back into a mental scenario of managing somebody or something. I notice that I feel more located and in charge when I am involved in that old, familiar mental exercise. Contemplating spiritual ideas, or just getting quiet can make the ego feel at sea, and therefore anxious. It takes a lot of loyalty to the good and a lot of practice to break reactive, interpersonal habits of thinking. But it's worth it. There is no stress or high blood pressure in Soul awareness.

Duty, Goodness, and the Divine Good

The insight about art as Soul activity has been facilitated over the last couple of years by discoveries from certain literary sources, especially two to which I have already referred: *Twenty Minutes of Reality* and the film and book *The Enchanted April.* My thinking about activity had been dominated by issues of duty and personal goodness, and these are discussed in both works in greatly illuminating ways.

Margaret Montague discusses the issue of duty while she is pondering the implications of her bliss realization:

> In what I saw there was nothing seemingly of an ethical nature. There were no new rules of conduct revealed by those twenty minutes. Indeed, it seemed as though beauty and joy were more at the heart of Reality than an over-anxious morality. It was a little as though (to transpose the quotation),
>
> > I had slept and dreamed that life was duty,
> > But waked to find that life was beauty.
>
> Perhaps at such times of illumination there is no need to worry over sin, for one is so transported by the beauty of humanity, and so poured out in love toward every human being, that sin becomes almost impossible.
>
> Perhaps duty may merely point the way. When one arrives at one's destination it would be absurd to go back and reconsult the guide-post. Blindness of heart may be the real sin, and if we could only purify our hearts to behold the beauty that is all about us, sin would vanish away....
>
> Perhaps, too, this may be the great difference between the saints and the Puritans. Both are agreed that goodness is the means to the end, but the saints have passed on to the end and entered into the realization, and are happy.... The Puritan, on the other hand, has stuck fast in the means — is still worrying over the guide-posts, and is distrustful and over-anxious.
>
> It is like walking and dancing. One could never dance unless he had first learned to walk, or continue to dance unless walking were always possible; yet if one is too intent upon the fact of walking, dancing becomes impossible. The Puritan walks in a worried morality; the saint dances in the vision

of God's love; and doubtless both are right dear in the sight of the Lord, but the saint is the happiest.

The Puritan's "worried morality" is an ego concern; the saint's "vision of God's love" is Soul awareness. As Montague clarifies later on in her report, "we could not help but dance if we could see things as they are." I love her appreciation for the Puritan as well as the saint, for walking as well as dancing. All of us start out walking, and all of us start out thinking that goodness is personal. But how priceless the discovery that our goodness is already and always established in our Soul being, and that Life to that Soul being is a dance, not a dreary trudge.

The same distinction between personal goodness and the divine good is made in a delightful way by Elizabeth von Arnim in her book *The Enchanted April.* In the story Lotty and Rose, two dutiful, self-sacrificing, and miserably unhappy London wives, escape to an Italian castle for the month of April. The first morning Lotty opens the shutters to a sun-spangled view of the Mediterranean. The beauty floods her consciousness, filling her with bliss:

> It was as though she could hardly stay inside herself, it was as though she were too small to hold so much of joy, it was as though she were washed through with light. And how astonishing to feel this sheer bliss, for here she was, not doing and not going to do a single unselfish thing, not going to do a thing she didn't want to do.
>
> According to everybody she had ever come across she ought at least to have twinges. She had not one twinge. Something was wrong somewhere.... At home she ... had been so good, so terribly good, and merely felt tormented. Twinges of every sort had there been her portion; aches, hurts, discouragements, and she the whole time being steadily unselfish. Now she had taken off all her goodness and left it behind her like a heap of rain-sodden clothes, and she only felt joy. She was naked of goodness and was rejoicing in being naked. She was stripped and exulting.

Freed from the demand to subserve other people's needs and wants, she is freed as well from the physical and emotional fruits of such an inauthentic mentality. Not only does she lose her aches and pains and depressions, but she can no longer even picture her rigid, domineering husband.

> She simply could not see him as he was. She could only see him resolved into beauty, melted into harmony with everything else. The familiar words of the General Thanksgiving came quite naturally into her mind, and she found herself blessing God for her creation, preservation, and all the blessings of this life, but above all for His inestimable Love; out loud; in a burst of acknowledgement.[36]

Lotty's spontaneous verbalization of the Prayer of General Thanksgiving illustrates Montague's assertion that we cannot help but dance when we see things as they are, that is, with Soul eyes instead of ego eyes. We live what we see. Soul seeing takes care of behavior and activity.

As long as we think about activity issues from an ego perspective, we cannot help but run into various "shoulds" and "shouldn'ts" from outside "authorities" such as family, church, or school. Personal rebellion is no solution, because rebels are as determined by that which they rebel against as are conformists. And anyway, the beliefs upon which personal choices are based are not the truth of our being. *There is no free choice on the ego level, because we did not choose the ego identity, and it runs the show within its own viewpoint.* Paradoxically, the more we understand that we have no life of our own apart from the divine, the more unique and original our lives become.

Principles of Soul Activity

I've had much opportunity to watch how spiritual understanding works in my own experience and that of family, students, and friends. We can contrast three characteristics of ego activity with three principles of Soul activity: (1) ego fantasy versus spiritual awareness, (2) insistence versus readiness, and (3) effort versus unfoldment.

1. *Ego Fantasy versus Spiritual Awareness.* When we start to think about what we want to do, either as young adults just starting out or older adults wanting to make a change, the ego jumps in immediately

with its fantasies. The trouble with such fantasies is that they are de-termined to some degree by negative beliefs about ourselves. Like the man mentioned above, who was sure he knew how to make his dreams come true, it is likely to be the negative beliefs that give rise to the fantasies that take form. Or, if the fantasies are realized, we may find our limited sense of ourselves having a hard time coping with the situation. We all know the saying, "Beware of what you set your heart on, for you may get it." There's a reason why something we think we want is not yet in our experience. Knowing this leads to the next distinction between ego and Soul activity.

Spiritual awareness transcends the limits of ego identity. In the awareness of the universal, spiritual substance of Life, the negative beliefs about ourselves are gradually refined away. This appears as our experience becoming less troublesome, conflicted, or impeded. We feel healthier, more centered, and happier. And things happen that are better than we could ever have cooked up for ourselves.

2. *Insistence versus Readiness* Whenever I feel a sharp insistence about something, I now know to be alert, because it means that ego is pushing its agenda. The insistence indicates that it is pushing against itself, against some contradictory inclination that it doesn't want to ad-mit. The insistence to myself that I just *had* to get married masked, as I later discovered, an underlying fear of marriage that was secretly in-sisting that I just had to *not* marry. So insistence is best responded to as evidence of a need to wait and to work in consciousness until readiness releases the ego insistence.

Readiness is a wonderful quality of life that shows up very clearly in the development of children. We watch as our babies and toddlers eagerly, effortlessly move on to each stage of development the moment they are ready for it. Readiness is the principle that no positive step needs to be forced, because Life is expressing itself in perfect harmony with Its own nature.

Seeing readiness manifest in our children's experience helps us to let it govern our activity as well. When personal sense is insisting, "But I want this now. . . . I am ready for it," I often remind myself, "If you were ready for it now, it would be in your experience now." We do not have to make Life obey us, which is what ego, unwittingly, tries to do. Life is perfectly obedient to Its own nature; Soul is the awareness of that nature; and right activity expresses itself from that awareness.

But what can we do if we want to become ready for something that apparently we're not ready for yet? We can increase our readiness for a higher form of the good by consciously translating personal wants into the spiritual qualities that are the truth behind the wants. If we want better work, a better house, better anything, the "better" implies greater quality. So we then consider the qualities that such work or such a house would embody. Right now my husband and I are contemplating a move to a different location. As we think about a new home, we consider it in quality terms: more privacy, more of the beauty and harmony of nature, more interesting and useful space in the house. We work in consciousness by recognizing as already present the qualities that we want the new house to embody. We dwell in "the secret place of the Most High," where beauty, grace, freedom, harmony, and peace are already fully established. Dwelling in the spiritual substance is the best way to allow that substance to take form, in its own good time, as a particular house in the right location. "You've got to have home in your heart...."

3. *Effort versus Unfoldment.* One of the catchwords of our day is "stress." To personal sense, everything is difficult. Believing ourselves to be, so to speak, "battery operated" rather than "plugged into the Source," and believing that life is everlastingly a matter of managing self and others, we feel stressed. It is worth noticing, however, that it is these beliefs that feel stressed. The "cause" of the stress is subjective, not objective.

Ego is matter-based identity that brings with it a host of opinions about activity. A young wife and mother, to whom the term "housewife" signifies a trap that would result in a complete loss of her creative integrity, describes how that belief inhibits her capacity to even pick up a sock from the floor: "If I pick up one thing, then I have to pick up everything else, and before you know it, I'm spending my days picking up dirty clothes and doing laundry. And if I get used to that, my dreams will die off and I won't even notice or care. I will have sold out to society's definition of 'wife.'"

This woman's painful quandary illustrates again that the issue is never the behavior or external factors; the issue is what those things mean in the context of ego identity. It is the mentality rather than the form of the activity that is all-important.

Another woman, who described herself as "a very ordinary woman" whose "days [are] given up to housework" reported an entirely different sense of her daily activities. She wrote:

> I [can] truthfully say that I have given way, day after day, to an ecstasy of wonder at the fresh clean water in my dishpan, and have stood, like a gaping idiot, sometimes for several moments, gaping at it as though it were Niagara Falls — and so it is, only a "little less." From the eternal mystery of the stars down to my very dishpan it's all so thrilling, so outside of ourselves, so God-put-together, that there has never been, to me, any "commonplace." . . . It seems perfectly unescapable, this endless consciousness of Joy and Beauty.[37]

"So outside of ourselves, so God-put-together" points to the sense of reverence that springs from her Soul focus on spiritual *substance* rather than an ego preoccupation with form. The Soul focus protects her from the loss of identity so feared by the housewife described above. Our true identity is maintained, eternally, in Soul. Personal identity is already, as we have noted, a betrayal of our true being, so the defense of its integrity is an altogether misguided cause.

John Hargreaves writes:

> [Working in consciousness] does not mean neglect of human duty, but it does ensure its more effective discharge. Living out from the divine sense of things, the duties of the human realm appear less arduous, and are carried out more by grace than effort. Our sense of duties changes. The feeling of being trapped in an endless round of demands that are imposed from outside yields as man is found to be the activity of the divine Mind, but not an independent actor. In fact duties are never the problem in themselves. It is the material sense of them that makes any burden, and this sense disappears before the conscious presence of divine, effortless Life.[38]

One of the most noticeable fruits of spiritual understanding in my life has been a gradual shift from tiresome, stressful work to relatively effortless activity that is no longer sharply divided into work and leisure. Since our sons left home, my days have an extraordinary peace, harmony, and solitude to them. The dread with which I awakened every morning for probably five decades has largely dissolved. There is very little that I "have to" do that can even seem to interrupt the quality substance of the day.

Money and Activity

Money is one of the knottiest problems in human experience. No matter how much we have of it, most of us have trouble with it. The most ordinary belief about it is that it is a medium of the good life that we must earn by certain activities. We notice a few people around us who have either inherited wealth or acquired it through inspired inventions or investments and seem to be freed from the preoccupation of earning it. But for most of us, the need to make money operates as the big determinant of and restriction on activity.

In one of the quotations opening this chapter, Jesus gives us a law of consciousness that I am only beginning to really understand and, therefore, to take seriously. "Seek first God's kingdom," he says. Seek the conscious awareness of the presence of divine Life *before* you take thought for what you will eat or drink or wear. Those things are incidental to the realization of the kingdom. "Fear not, little flock. For it is your Father's good pleasure to give you the kingdom." So there is no excuse for thinking that your well-being, on any level, is a matter of your personal effort and labor.

I am just beginning to see through the human beliefs about money and work enough to find myself having moments of breathless wondering. What if Jesus' famous sermon about the birds of the air and the lilies of the field is really true? What if our heavenly Father will feed and clothe us, not minimally, but abundantly, gorgeously, by way of our consciousness of His kingdom?

All the way along in this book we have discovered that the issues of life are *subjective*, in consciousness. It can't be different in terms of money. Money is a metaphor for support. Money seems to support and even enable us to live a quality life. But if quality Life is already established, and if "my life" is really just that one, universal quality Life manifesting Itself, then there cannot be a material requirement before it can be expressed. I begin to see that money is incidental to Life's flowering. It is just one form of the support that invariably accompanies a Soul idea's unfoldment. An idea that reflects quality Life already brings with it its support and nurture. As the idea clarifies, various forms of support show up as part of the blooming process. Money, if needed, will appear. But we must never assume that money is the means to the manifestation of a right idea.

A young mother of two was faced with foreclosure on her house after her divorce. The amount of the mortgage loan substantially surpassed the current market value of the house, so just selling it wouldn't solve the problem. She had also borrowed for the down payment, and that loan was still due. She faced the prospect of having to move in with her parents and of being catastrophically in debt. She was encouraged to claim her Soul identity as Life's fullness expressing Itself, with no possibility of a vacuum, lack, displacement or unmet need.

Although she had checked with the bank some months earlier and had been told that foreclosure was the only option, she phoned again. She was told of a new provision that under special circumstances would allow for the house's sale and the total forgiveness of any remaining debt. The lender of her down payment, a relative, notified her that repayment was no longer expected. She ended up being able to stay free in the house for some months during the process of the sale. During this time she was able to save up money for an apartment for herself and her children. She said, "It was just as if I woke up from a bad dream. The whole nightmare situation just dissolved."

The Gift of the "Big I"

I said at the beginning that this book is for those who want to move beyond the experience of life as problem solving. Years ago, though I scarcely knew what it meant, I found myself thinking, "Life is not a problem to be solved. It is a gift to be received." Not just individually, but collectively, we need to realize the giftedness at the heart of every aspect of living. This is especially crucial in coming to terms with the technologies that both bless and plague our society. Zen Master Shunryu Suzuki writes:

> If you think that God created man, and that you are somehow separate from God, you are liable to think you have the ability to create something separate, something not given by Him.

For instance, we create airplanes and highways. And when we repeat, "I create, I create, I create," soon we forget who is actually the "I" which creates the various things; we soon forget about God....

Because we do forget who is doing the creating and the reason for the creation, we become attached to the material or exchange value. This has no value in comparison to the absolute value of something as God's creation. Even though something has no material or relative value to any "small I," it has absolute value in itself. Not to be attached to something is to be aware of its absolute value....

But if we are aware that what we do or what we create is really the gift of the "big I," then we will not be attached to it, and we will not create problems for ourselves or for others.

And we should forget, day by day, what we have done; this is true non-attachment. And we should do something new.[39]

Material identity sees creation as personal and cannot help but be attached to it. We all have experienced, in one way or another, the negative side of personal attachments. Every "claim to fame" that bolsters our ego sense of achievement and importance also locates and limits us and keeps us looking to the past. Suzuki Roshi's charming description of everything as "the gift of the 'big I'" is itself a gift of the big I, that is, of Soul's viewpoint on Life.

The blissification of seeing promises to all of us ever greater clarity in the areas of experience in which we still feel blind and bumbling. The spiritual laws of the universe are optionless; the spiritual substance of the universe is inviolate; the spiritual identity of humankind is forever intact. It's just a matter of learning how to notice and of loving — *absolutely loving* — to see what Soul sees.

Soul Seeing Reports

Consistently in bliss reports there is a correlation between the momentary loss of personal ego identity and the ensuing Soul vision. In this report, Moyra Caldecott describes her experience when, as a "nervous, giggly schoolgirl," she was confirmed in her church:

The service went on and I, as usual, was only half aware of it. My mouth was opening and shutting, saying the expected words, but my thoughts were all over the place — certainly not on anything profoundly religious.

The time came for us to file up to the altar rail and kneel down. I did so. Not expecting anything. Noticing how prickly the kneeling cushion was on my knees. Waiting for the Bishop to reach me. He was muttering something and putting his hand on each one's head in turn.

It was my turn. He put his hand on my head...I didn't hear what he said but...

I suddenly ceased to be me (that is, in the sense of "me" I had thought I was — living in a particular house, in a particular street, going to a particular school). I felt the most incredible flow of energy and power coursing through me and had what I believe to be an experience of Timeless Reality...of consciousness that took in everything without limit...but reacted to nothing except in the sense of "knowing...and...loving."

The Bishop must have had his hand on my head for no more than a few seconds — but one could live a whole lifetime and not gain as much insight as I gained in this one beautiful, devastating moment.[40]

Of particular importance in this report is the revelation that Soul awareness, freed from the specifics of the ego lens, takes in "everything without limit" but reacts to "nothing except in the sense of knowing...and...loving." Nothing is lost in the loss of self-consciousness, except obscuring judgments. Since there is no sense of need, there is no utilitarian focus on what is seen. All is known and loved in its beingness. Humanly we are so used to feeling reactive to everything we see and hear that we probably don't even recognize what a loss of integrity and freedom such reactivity entails. As we savor bliss reports, we begin to feel the soaring joy of a cognition that sees everything in such holy beauty that it evokes only love and gratitude.

The following report points up that we "cannot serve two masters" in our thinking. The anonymous writer describes the experience as being "of a definite moral nature":

I believe I am naturally very honest, but at the time I speak of
I had been pursuing, for a considerable period, a course that
was, to say the least, disingenuous, and thereby I was attaining
what seemed to me at the time a great advantage. I was not
at peace, however, and all spiritual truth, to which I had previously been keenly sensitive, appeared to me dead and unreal.
I used to pray that I might be made to *feel* the reality of it,
but no answer came until, after a long time of jangling conflict
and inner misery, I one day, *quite quietly and with no conscious
effort*, stopped doing the disingenuous thing.

Then the marvel happened. It was as if a great rubber
band which had been stretched almost to the breaking point
were suddenly released and snapped back to its normal condition. Heaven and earth were changed for me. Everything was
glorious because of its relation to some great central life —
nothing seemed to matter but that life. While the experience
lasted...I could have gone cheerfully to the stake. I walked
on air, so gloriously commissioned did I feel by some higher
power. Even the details of daily living, such as tying one's
shoestrings, or brushing one's teeth, which had previously almost suffocated me by their monotony, became of thrilling
interest as fitting me for the work I was to do.

Reality was shown to me in answer to my prayer. I *saw*,
as plainly as I see the city chimneys from my window as
I write, great shoulders of Truth and Righteousness reach-
ing down underneath all material things like the rock-ribs
of a mountain-side beneath the shifting clouds and shadows. I saw that all material things are but clouds and shadows in comparison. Hence I have never doubted what *Reality* is.[41]

This testimony shows the way Soul triumphs over personal sense.
The ego cannot release itself. However much this individual might
have argued with himself or herself over behavior, the survival drive
of personal sense would continue to insist on the necessity of the behavior. The report suggests that it may be more fruitful to give up
wrestling on that level of thinking and to spend as much time as possible acknowledging Soul's view. This is seeking first God's kingdom,

and the kingdom then does its own work of releasing the personal agenda.

One of the things that bothers me in the current political emphasis on "virtues" is that the thinking never leaves the level of ego. That's why it all ends up so hypocritical and demoralizing. Egos cannot *do* virtue; it's not on their résumé. Bliss experiences make clear that virtue belongs to Life, not personhood, and it is something to be acknowledged, cherished, realized as the truth. Better for us all as persons to humbly confess that "we just don't know enough about love" than to think that our miniscule, puny personal goodness could ever qualify us for applause.

Even better than confession is a great big belly laugh. Here's a bliss equivalent, reported by a teacher of Transcendental Meditation.

> I had been sitting in a long and peaceful meditation. Or at least, most of it was peaceful, the initial stages had been preoccupied with a personal problem as to whether I should do one of two things. Otherwise there was nothing extraordinary about the meditation, except perhaps it was very still and more peaceful than usual. Afterward I lay down on the floor for a few minutes, as is my normal practice. Suddenly, for no apparent reason, waves of bliss and happiness started moving through my body. It was very much a physical sensation which seemed to come somewhere in the center of the chest.
>
> As they spread through my body I felt ridiculously happy, so much so that my inner smiles broke out into spontaneous laughter. I lay there laughing and laughing until suddenly the problem I had been immersed in flitted through my mind. It now seemed silly and insignificant; and anyway, either solution would be fine. The fact that I could have become so immersed in it just made me laugh more and more.
>
> Then my body started a dancing movement, if you can call it that. Lying on the floor the whole body began a series of movements rather reminiscent of Indian dancing. Arms, legs, hands, body, neck all flowing, waving and rippling completely spontaneously. This lasted for about ten minutes, gradually

subsiding and leaving me in a state of incredible peace and well-being.

Coming out into the garden the whole world seemed fresher and crisper, and much more immediate. The most interesting thing was that the problem I had been so pre-occupied with remained far away and insignificant — and in fact has never bothered me since.[42]

This report reminds me of a story about a Zen monk who upon en-lightenment was so stuck by the absurdity of the mortal misconception of things that he laughed for two days and two nights, nearly laughing himself to death! If our personal issues and worries can look so ludi-crous from the standpoint of real Life, then perhaps we can remember to hang loose a bit, even when they seem compelling. Perhaps we can be interested in finding that higher viewpoint that alone can release the grip of the ego concern.

CHAPTER 7

Soul and Society

Be noble, and the nobleness that lies in other men, sleeping, but never dead, will rise in majesty to meet thine own.

— LOWELL

And he that sat upon the throne said, Behold, I make all things new.

—REVELATION 21:5

Two Principles of Seeing

"Behold, 'I' make all things new." That "I" is Soul. Soul provides a new eye that, as we have seen, yields up a new identity. Soul's eye/I reveals the human being as God's spiritual image, and human affairs, individually and collectively, are then seen in a totally new light.

In considering the major issues of our culture, we can notice how the I/eyes of ego and of Soul operate. Ego eyes tend to fix upon what is wrong, and this activates what we may call "The Problem Focus Principle": *A conscious focus on what is wrong and bad confirms the beliefs that are expressed humanly as wrong and bad structures and behavior.*

The eyes of Soul operate in a way that can be stated as "the Soul Focus Principle": *The consciousness of what is right and good shows up on the human level as structures and behavior that are right and good.*

Soul seeing does not simply give us an alternative way of coming at human issues, one opinion among other opinions about society's ills and their solutions. If we take seriously that the human being *is* Soul rather than ego, then what we are *about*, collectively as well as individu-

129

ally, is totally different from what we have thought humanly. What we
are about is being the conscious manifestation of divine quality Life,
in all situations, at every moment. And it is from this standpoint that
we will now consider some of the major social issues of our day.

As the Soul Focus Principle clarifies, there is no way things can get
better in a seeming external world except as a reflection of an improve-
ment in the quality of consciousness. And the only place any of us can
have dominion is at the point where it calls itself *our* consciousness.
While social change can be brought about through force — violent or
nonviolent — real conversion in the hearts of men and women occurs
only from within. Being true to our own withinness is not only the
starting point but also the goal of Soul realization. There is only one
consciousness, and we deal with it here, not there.

We spoke in chapter 2 about the betrayal of Soul that takes place
in the very definition of ourselves as persons. Personhood defines us as
separate from the good, and we are then driven to seek it outside of
ourselves in other persons, places, and things.

Soul betrayal is evidenced daily in personal advice columns in the
papers. I note regularly letters telling of abuse in a relationship but of
the writer's inability to leave because, the writer says, "I love the person
so much." Clearly, that which would settle for abuse in the name of
"love" does not love and support itself. Soul sense, aware of Its quality
completeness, does not attract abuse in the first place and would not
tolerate it for a single moment, should it be exposed to it.

Though less dramatic, Soul betrayal is also reflected in the stream of
letters complaining of being taken advantage of by others — friends,
relatives, neighbors — and asking how to make them stop their behavior "without hurting their feelings." This concern with not hurting
others' feelings is not really a concern *for* others but a concern to be ap-
proved of *by* others. It doesn't make sense even humanly. Why should
we be concerned with the approval of people we think are rude and in-
considerate? Yet so unsure are we of our own values, so alienated from
a sense of inner integrity, that we allow and even invite the rudeness
that makes us fume and fuss.

Of central concern in our culture today is the demand for what
is termed "our rights." Virtually every shape and form of personal
identity demands that other shapes and forms give it its rights. Race,
ethnic origin, gender, age, disability, sexual preference, and virtually

every other conceivable form of special identity and personal belief is parading its right to...what? In the beginning, there was a legitimate concern with legal rights, but the focus has been lost in the metastasis that is now consuming so much of the energy of our society. The ego's inherent drive for self-confirmation has latched onto the idea that it can legally force others not only to recognize and respect its particularities but to produce whatever forms of recognition it may wish to demand.

I was recently talking with a woman who teaches third grade in a public school. I was commenting on a study that showed a continuing failure of children at fourth-, eighth-, and twelfth-grade levels to be able to write persuasively and to reason clearly. She said that there is a great emphasis in the curriculum on teaching writing skills, but that at least a third of the children in her class — a class in an affluent, middle-class suburb — seem unable to perform even the most minimal exercises. "We write in our journals every day," she said. "I give them topics that are really relevant to them such as, 'Write about what you do when you get home from school.' Yet some of them cannot write more than one or two sentences."

When I asked the teacher what she thought might be blocking the children who couldn't write, she said, "Those children seem only concerned about themselves, whether they are being noticed, getting attention. It seems that their minds are riveted on 'me, me, me,' and they have no interest in anybody else or in things outside themselves."

I then asked the teacher if in conferences with the parents of these children she noticed anything that might help account for the kids' self-centered focus. "These are the parents," she commented, "who are concerned only with their children's *rights* and whether *their* children's needs are getting met."

Once again, Soul betrayal reveals itself in the ego's very quest to get itself supported. Children of grade-school age are naturally curious, exploring, open to wonder in the discovery of the world around them. How tragic and telling that the Soul eyes of many such children are being shuttered by a preoccupation with the little personal self.

It is a misconception of identity that concerns itself with wresting attention and approval from others, even if it is seemingly for our children's benefit. Serving the ego agenda, we remain blind to the universe of quality good, and our children wander in a fog of self-concern.

In demanding that others recognize our ego rights, we give away our God-given Soul rights, and it is no wonder that we then feel hampered, frustrated, and impeded in our proper growth. Moreover, the mistake is likely to be compounded by then blaming others for not giving us the very thing we have ourselves betrayed and abandoned.

The Right to Be Whole

Demanding the right to be partial and separate in any of a number of specific ways, we relinquish the right to experience ourselves as whole. Claiming the right to behave in particular ways, we lose sight of our right to let the universal energies and qualities of Life express themselves through us in unimaginably fresh, inspired ways. Justifying adversarial thinking and behavior as necessary to the enforcing of our rights, we abandon our Soul eyes, the viewpoint that alone can fill us with the sweet sense of Life's omnipresent beauty and goodness. And, heartbreakingly, in letting our thinking be captured and run by self-centered concerns, we invite the discords, hostilities, and threats to our own and our children's well-being that fill us with such fear and despair.

Soul does not lead us to discount others, nor does it create conflict with others. Rather, it lifts us into a oneness with others from which harmonious and mutually beneficial activity can result. Jesus said, "Seek *first* the kingdom of God and these things shall be yours as well." We can trust Soul to protect and bloom us when we love ourselves enough to seek *first* our spiritual, quality identity, the kingdom already established within.

Soul Integrity and Politics

In recent elections the oft-repeated theme was, "The voters are angry." Those running for office tried to play to that anger and utilize it for their campaigns with scathing accusations against their opponents. We heard again and again, "Negative campaign ads work, however much we may all hate them." But for whom do they work? By the end of the campaign, there was an overall sense of disgust. The most basic values of a wholesome society seemed nowhere in evidence.

In her *Newsweek* column, Meg Greenfield exposed what she called "the giant, controlling lie that is at the heart of most [politicians'] arguments." This lie, she stated, is that "the American people can have...pretty much everything at no additional cost, possibly even at a saving, maybe *without even paying at all!*" She went on to suggest a "revolutionary idea" to those seeking office: "Since the electorate appears not only to punish those who tell the truth about these things, but also, in eventual outraged disappointment, to punish those who don't, why not tell the truth? Politicians, think about it. They're going to get you anyway, and this way you might even get into heaven, or at least get your self-respect back here on earth."[43]

I was struck by the insight of her analysis, which revealed that Soul betrayal operates in politics just as it does elsewhere. Trying to manage our lives by manipulating other people's thinking and behavior, we not only get rejected by the others in the end, but we have sold our self-respect and blocked our entrance to heaven, Soul awareness. I would only add the voters to Greenfield's call to integrity. Voters are as responsible for their unrealistic expectations as the politicians are for appealing to them. Each voter, like each politician, exercises responsibility at the point of choosing ego calculation or Soul integrity. If we choose ego calculation, we are assured that it will betray us.

In this article Greenfield illustrates constructive social commentary. She takes a look at the underlying issues that are the source of the difficulties for both sides rather than just announcing her personal bias. The article addresses issues, needs, and values rather than verbalizing a particular personal viewpoint and agenda.

It is of crucial importance that we distinguish social criticism based upon clarifying insights from that based on ego opinions. Sure, it feels great when somebody, especially somebody who seemingly *is* somebody, voices an opinion that supports our own. It feels as if there's somebody "on our side." But maybe the real issue is being on Soul's side. Rather than reveling in the support of others for our arbitrary little ego prisons, we would do better to cherish a viewpoint that can help us get beyond all partisanship.

Think about it: wouldn't it make sense to reward with our support and interest the voices of clarity and intelligence in our society rather

than the voices of ego judgment and self-righteousness? To reward
those who promote devils in our thinking is evidence that we have betrayed Soul by allowing the ego perspective to determine our interests
and values.

Soul seeing offers us something preferable to cultural and political
opinionatedness. It gives us the capacity to discern and enjoy truthfulness wherever it shines through the voices of ego, on all sides of every
issue. Soul discernment is expressed humanly as a desire to share with
one another helpful insights that potentiate the Soul wisdom of the
entire culture. The "Ninth Insight" in *The Celestine Prophecy* speaks of
just such a shift in society:

> We're here on this planet not to build personal empires of con-
> trol, but to evolve. Paying others for their insights will begin
> the transformation. [Eventually we will be] getting paid for
> evolving freely and offering our unique truth to others.[44]

In a Soul-based society, the evolution of consciousness is the primary
concern, and social structures that serve that end are the ones that
thrive.

Mental Pollution and Our Right Not to Know

Signs are already in evidence that the culture is waking up to the issue
of mental pollution. Just as the belief that smoking was an individual
issue that was nobody else's business has yielded to the recognition that
residual smoke is harmful to those who breathe it, so our mental indi-
vidualism is being called into question. The beliefs that what we think
is private, that our values are nobody else's business as long as we don't
physically encroach on others, and that everything is okay "between
consenting adults" are proving themselves mistaken. The media bring
home to us continually that we live in a common mental world. Nothing is private anymore, and privacy as a value seems to have virtually
disappeared. Intrusiveness is the operating value of the news media
and of sales strategists. The public has so succumbed to media mes-
merism that many people clearly believe that exposing — and watching
others expose — their grotesque and pathetic misconceptions about life
on national TV is of value.

When we understand that only God's universal qualities and values are life-enhancing and health-producing and that these qualities and values must be claimed and cherished in consciousness, our perspective on "the right to know" changes dramatically. We now begin to realize that Soul identity operates as our "right *not* to know" the pictures that the carnal mind is peddling. Mental pollution is far more toxic and detrimental to the public welfare than second-hand smoke.

The recognition of the fact and danger of mental pollution heightens fears and may foster the drive for tighter censorship of films and literature that are deemed toxic. But as the Problem Focus Principle warns, a fearful concern with managing negative influences tends to reinforce them.

What is needed is not a management of the bad but new eyes, Soul eyes, that can see the universe of spiritual good. Only as Soul identity reveals a far, far better good than the compulsive pursuit of self-destructive ego appetites can those appetites and the vast, cancerous social structures that feed, and feed upon, those appetites be healed.

Applying the seeing principles to the issue of censorship, we discover that the focus on unwholesome aspects of our culture becomes itself unwholesome. Filmmakers, writers, and performance artists who believe that the evils of society are corrected by being graphically portrayed don't understand the nature of consciousness. We don't discover the "extravagant beauty and importance" of every living thing by filling consciousness with images of horror and ugliness. The central issue of our lives is what we choose to let fill our minds. If we savor images that are the denial of spiritual good, it should not surprise us that we have experiences that deny the presence of spiritual good.

This does not mean that the "devilish" consequences of ego-based concerns cannot be shown in a way that educates and enlightens viewers. We could use a good deal more exposure of the connection between the beliefs and values of individuals and societies and the experiences that result from them. It is possible to portray all aspects of the human scene in a way that tends to relieve rather than stimulate negative states of consciousness. In our culture, there is far too much stimulation of rather than relief of personal sense. Ugliness, lust, horror, and brutality are shown for the titillation of the audience. Being scared, excited, and sexually aroused are considered to be positive experiences simply because they make us feel alive, on the physical/emotional level. Organismic excitement, however, is an amoral "good" that quickly goes bankrupt as the individual and collective price goes higher. An appetite for thrills is never satisfied, and its pursuit deadens an appreciation of the quality good that alone can ultimately satisfy. Bliss reports reveal the exquisite feeling of aliveness that accompanies Soul's quality awareness. Physical sensation is a poor counterfeit of spiritual vitality.

As a nation we simply cannot afford the naiveté that thinks that we can enjoy visions of violence, horror, ugliness, sensualism, and self-gratification as entertainment without inviting those things to dominate our individual and collective experience. Murder, rape, vandalism, drug use, domestic violence, emotional and mental illness, and many forms of physical disease directly reflect the devils that masquerade as "entertainment" and "news" in the ever-expanding flood of media offerings.

There is a recent surge of interest in trying to induce shame into people's thinking as a curb to negative behavior. While it is true that there is a remarkable lack of moral sense in our culture, shame is not the answer. Just adding another negative to our thinking won't do the trick. The subjective sign of Soul's inner Presence is a sense of *reverence*. Reverence reflects an underlying recognition of the divinity of all life. In the presence of reverence, the toxic beliefs that yield up immorality, selfishness, prejudice, and hate are self-seen and "sink abashed out of sight." Rather than trying to add shame to the poisonous stew of ego concerns that is making our society sick, we need to discover the Soul reverence that finds the whole stew totally unappetizing. Again, it is the consciousness of what is right and good that automatically, effortlessly is expressed as positive human experiences and structures.

Consciousness is the only place where we can know God and where we can come home to our own holiness. "Blessed are the pure in heart [consciousness]," said Jesus, "for they shall see God." If we would see God rather than devils, we will need to give up settling for devilish self-indulgences. It is only because we are so unaware of our inner kingdom of spiritual good that we fall for the fleeting "goods" of ego, which so consistently betray and discourage us.

Soul Safety

Our culture is preoccupied with safety concerns. Thinking that the threat lies outside of ourselves, we dash around locking doors, putting bars on windows, and screaming to imprison criminals and throw away the key. But as we have seen, our primary enemy lies in accepting personal identity and thus abandoning our Soul base within. William Law, a seventeenth-century Anglican cleric, wrote:

> You are under the power of no other enemy, are held in no other captivity, and want no other deliverance, but from the power of your own earthly self. This is the one murderer of the divine Life within you. It is your own Cain that murders your own Abel.[45]

Safety, like everything else, is subjective, not objective.

Hora says, "Nothing comes into experience uninvited." This is not to say that we consciously want bad things to happen but simply that it is our beliefs and values that open the door to what we experience. If we don't like what we are experiencing, it can be useful to inquire into "the meaning" of the experience. The meaning refers to the beliefs and values that are "inviting" the experience. Even young people can learn to relate their experience to their thinking.

Once when our sons were teenagers, they spontaneously healed a difficult situation in this way. They and some friends had become accomplished dancers, and they developed several group routines. They would go to discos on the weekends and dance, and often other groups of boys would challenge them to "a comp." Then they would compete, each group strutting its stuff to a circle of onlookers, whose response would determine the winners.

Our boys and their friends got the idea of wearing a kind of group uniform. They bought red sweat pants and shirts and had their group name emblazoned on the shirt backs. Of course, my husband and I, doting parents, thought they looked adorable and encouraged their project. But the night they first wore their uniforms, they came home very early and quite disappointed. They reported that the moment they stepped in the door of the first disco, they were accosted by a gang of boys who issued a very hostile challenge to a comp. They complied, trying to keep the competition playful and fun. But they found the others taking it very seriously and becoming quite belligerent and threatening. So they left and decided to come home.

The next day, Tom and Erik sat in the living room discussing the events of the previous evening. I joined them, only listening. They pondered together what could have accounted for the unusually aggressive and hostile approach of the other group. They concluded on their own that their flashy costumes were a form of drawing attention to themselves that other guys might interpret as bragging: "Look at what hot stuff we are!" This would make other male teenagers immediately defensive and eager to put them down. They realized that they could not have a casual evening of enjoyable dancing if they came onto the scene proclaiming their superiority. They felt great relief at identifying the meaning of the disturbing incident and decided never to wear the costumes again. There was no repeat of the unpleasant experience.

It might be worth noting that their decision not to wear the uniforms was based upon their desire to enjoy recreational dancing. They had no desire to become performers. Nor were they concerned with their "right" to wear whatever they wanted, in which case they might have chosen to continue to wear their uniforms and deal with the hostile interaction that was bound to come up. Indeed, if a macho value system had prevailed, they might even have enjoyed this form of "picking a fight" everywhere they went. But they just wanted to have fun dancing, so that value determined their response.

Personal sense typically promotes values and behavior that are inherently discordant and then blames others or society for the ensuing discord. Yet the lawful nature of the universe is untouched and will keep us safe if we honor it. Anybody willing to *ask*, rather than *tell*, Life how It works can come to understand and be supported by the divine laws of good. But we cannot break universal laws in consciousness and still expect them to support us in experience. Safety lies in being in conscious harmony with divine law, and this is the natural condition of Soul.

Soul identity *is* protection in a self-centered world. On several occasions, Jesus' life was threatened by an angry mob, yet he remained untouched and simply left the scene. In two reports, in Luke 4:30 and John 8:59, it even says that he went "through the midst" of the mob. Others have had similar experiences, one of which is referred to later in this chapter. These stories illustrate that the personal level of thought cannot see or interact with divine reality. When we remain on the same level of thought as the threat, either by fighting it or by running from it, we remain vulnerable to it. But Jesus, dwelling in divine Mind's awareness, literally became invisible to those around him, because there was nothing in his consciousness with which their viewpoint could interact.

A Litigious Society

We are all aware that we live in possibly the most litigious society in the world. The meaning of the word "litigious" is, first of all, "given to carrying on lawsuits," but second, "quarrelsome." The quarrelsomeness of our society is rooted in the current concern with ego rights. On the surface it appears to express a legitimate refusal to be victimized by other people. If we think we have been wronged by another, we have legal redress. We "don't have to take it lying down."

The underlying issue is dominion, and that, we have discovered, is ours, but not where ego says it lies. Dominion is ours in and as Soul identity. The preoccupation with rights on an interpersonal level leads to a mentality of victimization, as the Problem Focus Principle predicts. In the very process of suing the other, one remains — and must remain — a victim of the other, and the other must be seen as blameworthy, wrong, bad. Without a mentality of victimization and interpersonal blame, there is no legal case. But that mentality is the real victimizer of us all, and it cannot be healed in a court of law, even if financial restitution is obtained.

This is not to say that there are not legitimate lawsuits. Law, seen as the human representation of universal laws, is a necessary and laudable structure of society. There are times when a lawsuit may represent one's highest appreciable sense of the good. But such action should be based on principle — on a recognition of the already rightness of our Soul situation — not on personal reasons of blaming or revenge.

What is being addressed here is an unwholesome and misguided cultural value that reflects an ego refusal to own one's experience. This mentality prefers to blame others rather than face up to the ignorant beliefs that are inviting the problems. We have become an exceedingly "touchy" society, reacting with a mentality of angry reprisal to everything that displeases our egos at any moment.

The Value of Despair

In addition to being the most litigious society, ours may well be the most depressed society ever. And there is a secret, mental connection between depression and the compulsion to force people to change or "pay up" in court that is worth investigating. The connection shows up in considering an important psychological distinction between depression and despair. Psychologist Andras Angyal, a colleague of Abraham Maslow who was doing his own highly original work in the 1950s, writes of the importance of despair in the psychotherapeutic process. Though he speaks in terms of "neurosis," his comments apply to the ego lens in general as we have been discussing it.

> [Despair is] a sweeping experience of bankruptcy [that] must come if the person is to break out of his neurotic enclosure and take a chance on a different mode of existence which at first is unfamiliar and frightening.... The bankruptcy of neurosis need not be shattering when the hope for something else is clearly there.
>
> Unlike despair, depression has a tenacious quality and indicates that a profound attachment to the neurosis exists.... The patient proclaims, as it were, that his way is the only way, that he does not want to play the game differently.[46]

"Despair," as here defined, is the actual, mental release of the ego beliefs and their agenda, whereas "depression" is the state that arises when an individual sees the failure of the agenda but is still captivated by its insistence. Depression can lead to suicide; despair, in this definition, opens the door to new life.

I know from my own bliss realization that the loss of ego opens the door to heaven. The Soul Seeing Report at the end of chapter 4, in which bliss followed the woman's conscious release of her "misery...all its selfishness, pride, and fear," confirms the same discovery. We have nothing to lose and everything to gain by seeing through the beliefs to which depression would keep us hostage. Let us despair of them once and for all! Understanding that the real issue in depression is the ego's refusal to release unworkable beliefs, drug therapy may be used to aid that release process rather than helping individuals get along while retaining the offending misconceptions.

Suing God

"Be not deceived," says Paul in Galatians 6:7. "God is not mocked: for whatsoever a man soweth, that shall he also reap. For he that soweth to his [ego] shall of the [ego] reap corruption; but he that soweth to the Spirit shall of the Spirit reap life everlasting." The dictionary says that "to sue" means "to appeal to, to petition, to beseech." The problem with suing other people is that, as we have noted, they have nothing of value to give us. If we are going to appeal to something, we might as well appeal to the Source of all good. Before we sue another, let us sue God and see whether God's righteousness is expressed as legal action or not. In all likelihood, if our appeal is sincere, we will find a far greater and less troublesome reward, as the following story suggests.

> A man was about to buy a cottage in a small country hamlet when, at the last moment, someone else offered a higher price and his own offer was rejected. Understandably, he was outraged. During a conversation with a practitioner it was agreed that, at a certain level, such things were immoral and should not happen. But it was also recognised that merely fulminating over the situation was unlikely to help. The man agreed that Principle was not showing a lack of integrity to itself, nor was Love depriving itself. He also agreed that, scientifically, his only yardstick was, "Would I, the one I, do this to Myself?" He promised to put everything to this test, and within a day or so another cottage in this small hamlet became available. In no time the deal was made, and his family was able to move in.[47]

The common denominator in litigation and depression is ego insistence on getting its own way. The common denominator in despair and in suing God is humility, the releasing of personal terms and personal insistence for the sake of a higher substance and law. This is real forgiveness, which is giving-for-ness: the *giving* up of ego insistence *for* the sake of Soul awareness. Though it feels to ego like a loss of control, it is the sacrifice of ego control for the sake of Soul dominion.

Some years ago, I began to notice that there were times when I continued to be upset and depressed about things that I knew I had the tools to deal with. Then I would ask: "Okay, ego, what mileage are you getting out of this?" In every case, it would turn out that the thing I was fretting about confirmed some central theme of my personal story. Then I would conduct an inner hearing on the subject: "Yes, Ann, I know that's how things have always seemed. But haven't you let that story cry its tears and grouch and grump through you long enough? Wouldn't you like to move on now to something better and truer?"

Beyond Reactive Hate

One of the toughest issues that good people face is that of reactivity. In the face of hateful actions by others, we often notice ourselves caught up in a reactive rage that is not different from the very thing we despise. The conscious desire to inflict suffering upon someone who has inflicted suffering on others, especially upon children or animals, arises in all of us. But noticing that our feelings are the very same as those that we so loathe in the other, we may well wonder if there isn't a better way.

The better way is the subjective way rather than the objective way. We can notice that the physical death of the villain, however convenient in plot resolution on stage and screen, does not result in less of the mentality of fear and hatred that is the problem. Dominion over evil lies in calling into question the framework of our thinking rather than in accepting and reacting from the sense of things that that framework creates.

The first step is to recognize that everything comes to us at the point of consciousness. The bad is seen to be, not a person, but the spoiler, the misconception of life apart from God. We deal with the spoiler here, in consciousness, not out there, in and as a bad person. It is the ego's inability to see beyond the material scene that creates the illusion that we are on our own and are therefore helpless in the face of terrible wrongs. And that inability, and its sense of helplessness, is the problem.

One friend, in dealing with negative pictures whether in her own experience or that of others, says to herself, "This is a picture of what life would look like if there were no God." Then she goes on to see what happens to that picture when she activates her best, highest understanding of God and of Life. Soul eyes must be claimed and utilized if we hope to get beyond ego reactivity. Every day each of us needs to realize afresh: The end of hate is now, here, in *my* thinking, or it is never and nowhere.

Evoking Nobility

"Be noble, and the nobleness that lies in other men...will rise in majesty to meet thine own," wrote Lowell. Taking our stand in our own Soul identity, we evoke Soul in others. Again we come back to being concerned with what kind of men and women we want to be rather than with monitoring, managing, and manipulating other people. Didn't Jesus tell us, a long time ago, to take the logs out of our own eyes before trying to pick the splinters out of the eyes of others?

Ego tends to label such subjective dominion "unilateral disarmament" and consider it unfair and foolish. Personal sense protests: "Why should I do all the changing, forgiving, transcending? Why shouldn't he or she have to do something?" To such questions I am wont to reply: "Just because another person doesn't know enough to take the elevator down from the tenth story and insists on jumping out the window and hurting himself, does it make any sense for you to do it as well?"

We say we want dominion, but ego is prepared to give it away to others without exception in order to run its agenda of self-justification and blame. Most of us have so little experience with addressing issues in consciousness that it may sound impossible. We just can't believe that it can work. But it works if you work it. Unless and until we give ourselves the chance to actually experience the potency of consciousness work, we cannot judge it at all. We can only say, "I don't know. I have never really tried it."

How we experience things depends entirely on what we think life is *about*. Life is either about ego identity or it is about Soul identity. Not both. "Choose ye this day whom ye will serve." There is no waiting for society to change before our lives can improve. Thinking that a change of political leadership, moving to a small town, putting our kids in a different school, or any other external shift will bring us "the good life" and keep bad experiences away is a delusion.

The heartbroken father of a toddler who was critically injured in the Oklahoma City bombing said, "People will look at the pictures of my son and see that this has to stop." But some members of the militant group implicated were reported to be celebrating the bombing and predicting an influx of new members. If we look outside of ourselves for release from evil, we have betrayed Soul and activated within the very demons that we so fear without. The helplessness and rage expressed in the bombing resonate throughout the ego universe, swamping the national consciousness. Even Andy Rooney could not come up with anything better than, "I'd like to kill the bastards."[48]

The kingdom of heaven is accessed here and now, in consciousness, or it is not. Society reflects, but does not determine, the mentality of its individual members. The buck stops here. And the good news is that right here, right now, each of us already knows and lives the Soul identity that, when appealed to and given free reign in our lives, can heal us and heal the world as well.

Soul Seeing Reports

Two bliss/healing testimonies, which I am not permitted to quote verbatim, address major social issues of our day. I encourage readers to look them up. The first is that of a young woman who simply walked out of a concentration camp in broad daylight after she realized the truth of spiritual identity. The other deals with a beggar boy in a third world country who was transformed by the writer's moment of spiritual insight. Because these reports illustrate the potency of Soul seeing in actually changing seemingly fixed external situations, they are of utmost significance (see *A Century of Christian Science Healing*, pp. 136–45 and 217–19; the book is available at any Christian Science Reading Room).

The following report shows how a sense of suffering changes in light of Soul's viewpoint. Looking back on a bliss experience, the writer shares her observations:

> My point of view was entirely changed. Old things had passed away and all had become new. . . . *Every longing of the heart was satisfied*, every question answered. . . . I loved infinitely and was infinitely loved! The universal tide flowed in upon me in waves of joy and gladness, pouring down over me as in torrents of fragrant balm.
>
> This describes an actual sensation. The infinite love and tenderness seemed to really stream down over me like holy oil healing all my hurts and bruises. How foolish, how childish, now seemed petulance and discontent in the presence of that serene majesty! I had learned the grand lesson, that suffering is the price which must be paid for all that is worth having; that in some mysterious way we are refined and sensitized, doubtless largely by it, so that we are made susceptible to nature's higher and finer influences.[49]

As this woman suggests, bliss requires that consciousness be "refined and sensitized," and suffering seems to be one way that refinement takes place. At least at the beginning, most of us are not aware enough of Soul to seek it consciously. But the more we understand of quality Life, the more we can "volunteer" for positive experiences that "refine and sensitize" us. We are driven by suffering only until we see enough of the spiritual good to be drawn by wisdom and love to our true Soul identity.

Responding by letter to the publication of "Twenty Minutes of Reality," an individual wrote:

> Subconsciously I feel [bliss] all the time, although my outer mind must be often occupied with things of everyday life. Sometimes I can walk along the street amid the noise and din and confusion of a great city, and yet to me that is merely a dream; the reality is the sureness and the grandeur and the glory of Life, the inexpressible love of God, and the sublime order of creation. . . .

I am convinced that this state of consciousness is the proper heritage of "Whosoever will" receive it in God's way, and think enough in terms of the universal purpose and plan to become acclimated to things celestial. I feel sure that...almost any person...can so greatly enlarge his concept of life that it will be like a chicken stepping from its shell into the sunlight and the world beautiful....

You can amplify every faculty of mind, heart and soul, and by developing each (through prayer and obedience) you develop more and more all the faculties whereby you may come into closer touch with the Great Reality.[50]

We would not expect to learn to play a musical instrument without many years of daily practice. We devote hours and days and years of thought and activity to physical fitness, proper diet, mental development, even to entertainment. Yet few people think they have time to spend in daily spiritual study, a pondering of ultimate issues, a conscious feasting on spiritual goodness. And anyway, it's "not cool," "not fun"; it's a "should," it's "religious," it's "boring." Or, even worse, it's "not realistic." It "doesn't take suffering seriously enough."

I can only speak for myself. I think that good is better than bad and healing is better than suffering. I am glad to know where to turn when the old ego stuff comes up and grabs my throat in fear and regret. I am grateful that the pictures of horror and evil that parade across the media screens and knock on the door of my consciousness can be met with Soul sympathy, which works to heal and forgive, rather than with ego sympathy, which can only sob its regret and sorrow.

Every moment of willingness to look beyond personal feelings and desires has been rewarded with glimpses of grace and goodness that are indescribably precious. I wouldn't trade all the goodies of this world — even the things my ego so frequently moans and groans that it has missed out on — I wouldn't trade any of those for the sweet breath of Soul that increasingly blissifies my daily living.

"Whosoever will...." Will you?

CHAPTER 8

Soul: Eternal Life Now

Then shall [we] press on to Life's long lesson, the eternal lore of Love; and learn forever the infinite meanings of these short sentences: "God is Love"; and All that is real is divine, for God is All-in-all.

—MARY BAKER EDDY[51]

The Death of Death

The concept of death, like the concept of birth, belongs to a material viewpoint. Understanding that consciousness is the substance and location of Life is certain to change the way we think about death. The experience of personal, bodily death belongs entirely to the ego identity package. As persons who were born, we are bound to die, and if we don't die too soon, we may become afraid of not dying soon enough. Managing death is a preoccupation of material personhood.

The term "mortal" is a synonym for material identity. Since the term means "dead" it reveals to us that from the standpoint of that identity we are already dead. "Mortal identity" means, literally, "dead identity"! The thoughts and feelings that belong to that sense of things are inherently deadly. John Hargreaves writes:

> Reducing all to thought, it is apparent that...beliefs, or thoughts which do not emanate from the divine Mind, do not have life, because they lack the essential ingredients of Truth. They are "death thoughts," and they lead in turn to their acute form called the grave. Such thoughts as fear, hate, dishonesty,

criticism, envy, lust, and so on, are death in slow motion, or creeping death.[52]

Mortal belief can never yield up real Life, either here or hereafter. And since all is consciousness, the transition to the so-called hereafter will not, automatically, take care of the mistaken identity belief and its death-orientation. The end of death is here and now, in consciousness, or it is never. The end of death comes about by the death of death, that is, by the release of the death-bound mortal identity and its "creeping death thoughts," in light of the Life awareness of Soul identity.

The Life of Life

Just as ego identity *is* death, already, so Soul identity *is* eternal Life, already, here and now. Concluding his comments on "creeping death," Hargreaves adds: "Thoughts, or ideas, such as joy, abundance, peace, love, are Life thoughts, and constitute immortality."

Eternal life is here and now, in consciousness, as Soul seeing re-places ego emotions with quality awareness. *Immortality is not the living on forever of a personal identity, but the loss of the belief that Life is personal.*

The nature of the transition that will come for all of us in the to-tal release of bodily identity is determined by the degree to which we find and celebrate real Life, here and now. The more we find and live our Soul names now, the less impact the final release of our human names and their embodiments will have. This helps us realize that death is never the issue. Life is the issue. Find Life, and death, as it is interpreted and feared/desired by ego identity, will fade from view.

Most people find the idea of heaven or eternal Life difficult to imagine. The more sensually and emotionally oriented we are, the more life apart from bodily personhood could only seem to be bland and boring, and nothing could be worse than an eternity of boredom. This was Margaret Montague's great dread as a child growing up in a Christian belief system. She wrote:

> As a child I was afraid of world without end, of life ever-lasting. The thought of it used to clutch me at times with a crushing sense of the inevitable, and make me long to run

away. But where could one run? If never-ending life were true, then I was already caught fast in it, and it would never end.... The picture that Heaven presented to my mind was of myself, a desperate little atom, dancing in a streak of light around and around and around forever and ever. I do not know what could have suggested such an idea; I only know that I could not think of myself caught there in eternity like a chip in a whirlpool, or say "round again, and round again, and round again" for more than a minute, without hypnotizing myself into a state of sheer terror.[53]

Montague's fearful fantasy can be understood if we remember Emily, the ten-year-old girl in the novel *A High Wind in Jamaica,* whose self-discovery was discussed in chapter 3. She realized that she was stuck in a particular bodily identity "for a very long time," that is, until she died. Had she been presented with the idea of eternal life she might, like Montague, have concluded that it meant living on, *as Emily,* for all eternity. This would turn the "mad prank" of mortal selfhood into an eternal awareness of imprisonment. However much we may cherish our selfhood and try to hang on to it, all of us also have many moments in which we think we'd give anything to get out of it. Eternal ego identity would be a "no exit" hell.

So the flip side of ego fantasies about death is that at times it seems like a welcome relief. Most of us have times of thinking of death as a surcease, at least, to the pain of personal selfhood. We can understand the poet who felt "half in love with easeful death." Only uncertainty as to what really happens after death keeps many people from seriously considering suicide. If we are to really get beyond the issue of death, we must get beyond not only the fear of it, but the desire of it as well. The bliss of Soul awareness lifts us out of negative and positive preoccupations with death.

"Enjoying" God Forever

Montague's dread of eternity was healed by her bliss realization. She describes the shift in her thinking:

This is how, for me, all fear of eternity has been wiped away. I have had a little taste of bliss, and if heaven can offer this, no eternity will be too long to enjoy the miracle of existence. But that was not the greatest thing that those twenty minutes revealed, and that did most to end all dread of life everlasting. The great thing was the realization that weariness, and boredom, and the questions as to the use of it all, belong entirely to unreality. When once we wake up to Reality — whether we do so here or have to wait for the next life for it, — we shall never be bored, for in Reality there is no such thing.

Chesterton has pointed out the power for endless enjoyment of the same thing which most children possess, and suggested that this is a God-like capacity. . . . I think it was the truth of this suggestion that I perceived in those twenty minutes of cleared vision, and realized that in the youth of eternity we shall recapture that God-like and child-like attribute which the old age and unreality of Time have temporarily snatched from us.

Eternal life is revealed to be "endless enjoyment of . . . the miracle of existence."

When I was twelve years old, I joined the Presbyterian Church. In the Confirmation class, I learned the Shorter Catechism. I remember only the question, "What is the chief end of man?" and its answer: "The chief end of man is to glorify God and enjoy Him forever." I remember thinking that I knew what it meant to glorify God but that I couldn't imagine what it meant to "enjoy" Him, let alone forever. God and enjoyment didn't seem to match up in my duty-ridden, twelve-year-old thinking.

Many years later, when our boys were grade-school age, we took them to the beach. We hadn't been to the beach for quite some time, and they were entranced. For two hours I watched as they explored every aspect of the scene to the fullest: the sand, the water — every conceivable way of being in, on, and under it — the waves, the water in the sand, the sand in the water, the rocks, and the warmth of the sun, as they lay basking in it between forays into sea and sand. At the end, I thought to myself, "Now I understand what it means to 'enjoy God.' It means to explore and enjoy every facet of Life to its fullest, the way the boys abandoned themselves to every aspect of the beach today."

At the end of her report, Montague comments:

> The veil was very thin in my garden one day last summer. The wind was blowing there, and I knew that all that beauty and wild young ecstasy at the heart of life was rioting with it through the tossing larkspurs and rose-pink canterbury bells, and bowing with the foxgloves....

"Rioting" and "bowing": To enjoy God is to riot in and bow to the fullness of quality Life, as much as possible, every moment. Children do it naturally, but not consciously. We must begin to do it consciously, and then we can rediscover the Soul identity to which it comes naturally. Clearly, with such an orientation to Life many of the fears and concerns that accompany growing old and facing death would be greatly reduced.

Soul and Age

One of the terrible prices we pay for accepting material identity is that it sentences us to old age. The more important physical attractiveness is to us, the more demoralizing it is to see our bodies reflect the mortal belief of old age. Sometimes, in pursuit of beauty we create ugliness. My son recently reported seeing two women, somewhere around the age of seventy, on the bus. "One was just your normal old lady," he said. "She had a wrinkled face and gnarled hands. But she looked sweet and motherly. She was nice to look at. The other one had apparently had many face lifts. Her skin was drawn so tight that her face looked like a skull. She had no lips left, so the lipstick was painted on the skin. It was horrible, grotesque."

Beauty is a divine reality, and if we seek it in Soul, age cannot deface it. But if we seek it in matter, we have already lost it. Eddy writes:

> Beauty is a thing of life, which dwells forever in the eternal Mind and reflects the charms of His goodness in expression, form, outline, and color....

The embellishments of the person are poor substitutes for the charms of being, shining resplendent and eternal over age and decay.

The recipe for beauty is to have less illusion and more Soul, to retreat from the belief of pain or pleasure in the body into the unchanging calm and glorious freedom of spiritual harmony.[54]

"The recipe for beauty" is also a recipe for eternal Life: "to have less illusion and more Soul." Paying attention to "the charms of being, shining resplendent and eternal over age and decay" certainly beats peering into the mirror and bemoaning every new wrinkle. The promise of Soul awareness really comes home when human identity declares us to be "over the hill." The inescapable imprints of mortal belief on the body provide maximum motivation to be "absent from the body and present with the Lord."

Germaine Greer, writing in *The Change*, speaks of how the human process of aging tends to facilitate what we are calling Soul awareness:

When you are young, everything is about you. As you grow older, and are pushed to the margin, you begin to realize that everything is not about you, and that is the beginning of freedom....

The discontent of youth passes when you realize that the music you are hearing is not about you, but about itself. The important thing is not you listening to the music, but the self-realizing form of the music itself. Then you begin to understand that beauty is not to be found in objects of desire but in those things that exist beyond desire, that cannot be...subordinated to any use that human beings can make of them....

The older woman's love is not love of herself, nor of herself mirrored in a lover's eyes, nor is it corrupted by need. It is a feeling of tenderness so still and deep and warm that it gilds every grassblade and blesses every fly. It includes the ones who have a claim on it, and a great deal else besides.[55]

Despite a certain outrage every time I look in the mirror, I would have to agree that there are some marvelous things about being an "older woman." Turning sixty has given me a freedom from many ego claims. I've paid my homage to egoAnn's scenario, gotten what she wanted, done what she considered to be her duty, eaten at the table of her envy and jealousy and inadequacy and regret. From now on, I'm here for the good stuff, the Soul stuff. If I'm going to stay, I'm going to play!

Making the Transition

Although a spiritual perspective leads attention away from the personal transition called death, it has also given me a way of looking at that transition that provides a standard, humanly. In observing a number of passings, it is evident that there is an element of subjective consent involved. That consent seems to be given for either positive or negative reasons. The positive release of the whole of our story identity comes about from a sense of fulfillment. The negative release comes when the mortal scene becomes just too painful or too wearisome.

To my thinking, consenting for negative reasons is the equivalent of getting kicked out of school, whereas the positive motivation equals graduating. From birth on, there are transitions that require ego releases. If we have developed fully on the previous stage, then we graduate, and the next stage is fuller and better. If we cling to the previous stage, then we get kicked out. But being kicked out doesn't give us a positive basis for moving ahead. We don't just stay the same. Our experience becomes increasingly narrow and marked by the mentality of "creeping death."

Letting "creeping death" drive us into the grave, either by illness, accident, or conscious suicide, does not solve anything. Since all is consciousness, there is no escape from the need for toxic beliefs to yield to Soul awareness. We can be sure that, while we can't take material things with us, we can and do take material beliefs with us. The Christian concept of Purgatory after death corresponds to Tibetan Buddhism's clarifying discussion of what takes place at the moment of bodily death. Sogyal Rinpoche writes:

> The dawning of the Ground Luminosity, or Clear Light, at the moment of death is *the* great opportunity for liberation.

... [But] only if we have really been introduced to the nature of our mind,...and only if we have established and stabilized it through meditation and integrated it [our divine nature] into our life, does the moment of death offer a real opportunity for liberation.

Even though the Ground Luminosity presents itself naturally to us all, most of us are totally unprepared for its sheer immensity, the vast and subtle depth of its naked simplicity. The majority of us will simply have no means of recognizing it, because we have not made ourselves familiar with ways of recognizing it in life....Though all our confusion dies in death, instead of surrendering and opening to the luminosity, in our fear and ignorance we withdraw and instinctively hold on to our grasping.[56]

If we do not love and consciously seek the light of spiritual consciousness "here," we will not automatically do so "hereafter." Bliss awareness is heaven. If we hope for heaven after death, we had better be interested in it here and now. Realizing that I cannot escape negative feelings by dying has helped me repeatedly to face up to and get on with realizing the truth of being here and now. Precisely because ego belief is so painful and sticky and tiresome, I don't want to take it with me, to be worked out in whatever form or shape may be involved. I refuse to be kicked out! I *will* graduate and, if possible, graduate summa cum laude!

Molly's Graduation

I have seen a friend graduate with honors. She was Molly Morgenroth, and we met her and her husband at the Orange County Friends' Meeting more than twenty years ago. Molly and "Morgan" were wonderfully mature and enlightened people, probably in their sixties, who when we met them were making a decision about their future. They would have nothing to do with retirement communities, but were uncertain what the next location and form of activity would be. They took a year to live and study at the Quaker Retreat Center in Pendle Hill, Pennsylvania, in order to find their direction. At Christmas, they came back and reported to the Orange County meeting. They were thriving. Molly was thrilled with an art class and both were greatly stimulated by the environment. Then, in February or March, we got word of Molly's death. I was stunned. It didn't seem to fit with her glowing enthusiasm at Christmas.

A few weeks later, Morgan returned and shared with us the wonderful story of Molly's passing. He reported that they had both had the flu, which was not unusual for them. Both led very busy lives, and it almost seemed as if once or twice a year they would get the flu simultaneously so that they could spend a week together in solitude. On this occasion, they were well cared for, with their meals being brought to their little apartment and lots of friends keeping tabs on them.

But on Sunday, Morgan reported, no one came, except to bring meals. This was unusual, but appreciated. "We sat in front of a big window which looked out on the woods, and we talked about our whole lives," he said. "By evening, we had reached the silence which is beyond silence." They went to bed, and the next morning only Morgan awoke. Molly had passed on.

In pondering her passing, Morgan remembered that the week before in the silent meeting Molly had risen and spoken, which was a bit unusual for her. She had said, "Speak, Lord, for thy servant heareth." Going through her things after her death, he had come upon a piece of paper on which Molly had written something like this: "An image: Morgan and I walk through a field, hand in hand. The children come toward us and greet us, and we talk together for a moment, and then move on. We come to a river, and realize that one of us must cross over it first, alone. And it is all right." It was evident that Molly had been working through the issue of her transition for some weeks before her passing.

At a subsequent meeting in remembrance of Molly, I expressed my gratitude for Morgan's report and Molly's example. From Molly I learned that death can be graduation, and I learned how to do it with honors. And it makes perfect sense. Why should "the end" be any different from any other aspect of living? Life is a series of graduations, if all goes well. And always, while there may be some regret at leaving behind cherished people, places, and things, the joy of the graduation and the thrill of new vistas outweighs the regret. And in fact the longer we live, the more we discover that nothing valuable is ever really left behind. Since the real good is spiritual, we take with us — keep, in consciousness — every intelligent idea, beautiful sight, blessed feeling, and rich experience we have ever had. The more of this "heavenly treasure" we build up, the more easily and gladly do we move on to new visions of eternal good.

The Eternal Lore of Love

Actually, talk about "passing on" is metaphorical. If all is consciousness, then reality never goes anywhere. But the beliefs obscuring ultimate reality — beliefs that include time and space — do "pass off." A funny little Zen story, which I read years ago, has increasing meaning for me. It is said that a Zen master — I forget which one — called his students to him to tell them that he would die within the next few days. One of the students was weeping because his beloved master would be leaving them. The master replied, "Why do you weep? I am not going anywhere. Where would I go? It is only that when you call my name I will not answer."

Where, indeed, would we go? If ego is essentially a misconception about what is actually and already Soul, then there's nobody to go anywhere. The misconception dissolves, revealing that there has never been any life or mind but the divine Life and Mind. So "beliefs pass off, but 'I' do not pass on." The more we identify with Soul's "I," the less sense there is of a big crisis of transition coming up in the future.

We find ourselves brought back yet again to the fact that the only issue there is, ever, is that of consciousness, here and now. Eternal life is a state of consciousness, here and now, that is Soul-determined. Actually, we all have many moments of eternal Life every day, but we may not have learned to notice them.

Every time any quality comes to your notice, that's eternity shining through the graffiti of mortal belief. Every time you think, "How intelligent, how sweet, how beautiful, how charming," you are being Soul awareness recognizing Itself. Looking into a baby's face, you smile and say, "How cute." That's the innocence and purity of your Soul being enjoying Itself. Feeling a brisk breeze in your face, you think, "How refreshing." That's the freshness of divine Life recognizing Itself. When you sit with your loved ones in a moment of companionship and affection and think, "It doesn't get any better than this," that's the completeness of being celebrating itself. And it doesn't get any better than that: the conscious awareness of the good of God, here and now, in appreciable form.

In the quotation that begins this chapter, Mrs. Eddy speaks of "the eternal lore of Love." Such daily moments of quality enjoyment are that lore, already being "learned," that is, being recognized. I love the idea that the activity of eternity is that glad recognition of "the infinite meanings of ... 'God is Love' and All that is real is divine, for God is All-in-all." Anyone who has been a spiritual student for a substantial time knows the peculiar delight of rediscovering the same truths again and again, each time with deeper understanding. I laugh when I remember that when I first began studying with Dr. Hora, he told a story in which it took an ancient Chinese gentleman three years of mind fasting in order to become enlightened. I thought, "Three whole years! What a terribly long time!" It has now been nearly thirty years, and I am still, seemingly, *en route*.

But the route isn't really trying to get somewhere, like the ego always claims to be. It is really the delightful activity of feasting ever anew on "the endless lore of Love." Scarcely a week passes that I do not relish some new, deeper Soul insight. Each time I think, "So that's what that means. And I thought I understood it before." This suggests to me that indeed the meanings of the lore of Love are infinite and may be realized afresh eternally. That activity is, we could say, "what the angels in heaven do," rather than sitting on clouds and playing harps! It is Soul being actively aware. It "goes on" everywhere, all the time, and is, in truth, all that is ever going on, everywhere.

Just before her comments about "the eternal lore of Love," Eddy describes "man's spiritual progress," the end of which she describes in the following way:

> Then shall he drink anew Christ's cup, in the kingdom of God — the reign of righteousness — within him; he shall sit down at the Father's right hand: *sit down;* not stand waiting and weary; but rest on the bosom of God; rest, in the understanding of divine Love.

As I read these words, my inner response is a resounding "Yes!" I love the "*sit down*" — in italics. Yes, that "waiting and weary" stand-

ing about and seeming never to get really *there,* seeming never to
arrive, to be fulfilled and complete, that's what Soul awareness promises to deliver us from. Soul is "the reign of righteousness within" that
kisses our lives daily with glimpses of bliss. This is completion without stagnation, wholeness that includes endless variety and wonder. It
is eternal Life, as close as a baby's smile, as near as the fragrance of
a rose.

Soul Seeing Reports

One of the most interesting and informative healing reports I have
ever read is one that involves restoring a seemingly dead individual to
life. Medical technology in our day makes such returns of "clinically
dead" people not unusual and provides us with the increasing lore of
near-death experiences. But this report by Mary Baker Eddy of her
healing of a child is unusually revealing of the fact that death is a consciousness issue and of how mortal identity insists on itself, even to
the death.

> When living in Lynn, the four and a half year old boy of one
> of my students was taken seriously ill with what was called
> brain fever. He had been a little tyrant. The mother cared
> for the child without avail, and at length came running to my
> home with the baby in her arms.
> When she came in, she placed him on the bed saying, "I
> am afraid I have come too late. I think he is gone." And to all
> appearances the sick child had ceased to live. I told her to leave
> me and not to return for an hour.
> After her departure I went to God in fervent prayer and
> very soon the boy sat up in bed. I told him to jump down and
> come to me. He came and I took him in my arms and was
> silently declaring that he was not sick, when I saw the little
> fellow double up his fist and strike at me saying, "I *is* tick, I
> *is* tick." Although he struggled and fought in my arms, love
> prevailed, and he was soon at play with some spools that I had
> made into a cart with a darning needle. I still continued treat-
> ing him and again he came to me and struck me with his fist,

saying, "I *is* tick, I *is* tick." Then I said, "You are not sick and you are a good boy." Then he fell at my feet limp and lifeless, and I took him in my arms and my thought went out to my heavenly Father. The boy soon returned to consciousness and was ready to play again.

When I saw his mother coming, I told him to go to the door to meet her. When she opened the door and found her child healed, she was so overcome that she nearly swooned and I had for a time another patient. On the way home her little boy talked of God and said how good God is.[57]

The child's human identity sense included both sickness and badness. He "had been a little tyrant." Mrs. Eddy appeals to God, to the truth of the one Life, and the little boy is up and about. But when she mentally addresses the belief in sickness directly, it asserts itself. Children being less sophisticated than adults, the belief speaks directly through him, insisting that "I *is* tick," and hitting Mrs. Eddy. This is an illustration of self-confirmatory thinking, as discussed in chapter 5. The self insists upon its beliefs, without any concern with whether they are good or bad. Mrs. Eddy continues to realize the truth silently, and the belief, "hearing" itself addressed, protests again. Then she speaks aloud, in words that a child can understand, the truth of him: "You are not sick and you are a good boy." These ego beliefs are destroyed by the direct assertion of truth and for a time seem to take the child with them. But Mrs. Eddy again appeals to the "heavenly Father," the Author of true identity, and the child is restored, but without the ego claims of being sick and bad.

Not a word has been spoken to the child about God, yet with the release of the false identity sense Soul awareness fills his thought, and he speaks to his mother on the way home of "how good God is."

This lovely story has been an inspiration to me ever since I first read it. Often when I become aware of some personal belief insisting on its miserable feelings, I think of the little boy, with his doubled-up fist, shouting "I *is* tick, I *is* tick!" Then I can spot the spoiler at work and can "agree with [my] adversary quickly": "Yeah, yeah, I know all about what your claims are. But you cannot keep on masquerading as my thinking and feeling, because I know better. Soul tells me what I am, not you."

I am also inspired by Mrs. Eddy's calm, steadfast appeal to God and her trust in the power of the truth, no matter what the dramatics of personal sense. I have learned myself in many years of spiritual practice not to be discouraged if negative feelings or conditions do not seem to yield right away to consciousness work. I have come to see that every single appeal to God, every moment spent humbly acknowledging spiritual good as the truth of things, counts more than we can imagine. "More things are," indeed, "wrought by prayer than this world dreams of."

Although most bliss realizations seem totally spontaneous, others are clearly invited by conscious attention to God. Such was the case in the following report.

> I was in bed at the time it happened, and my elder son, then aged sixteen, was very ill with congestion of the liver. I lay there for some time worrying about him, and then realised that no good could come of that state of mind; so I deliberately set to work to relax and reverse each fear-thought. Finally, I was meditating on God using the words, "Be still, and know that I am God," and lingering mentally on what was implied by these wonderful words. Suddenly I became aware of a super-real state of being, with a completely relaxed feeling of blissful peace and trust in a Power of supreme beneficence and perfect harmony. One felt at one with it all and yet retained one's individuality....
>
> The state also includes a feeling of coming home after weary wanderings, being surrounded by the welcoming warmth of loved and loving ones — only of course greatly intensified....I have no idea how long it lasted, but its significance for me has been incalculable and has helped me through sorrows and stresses which, I feel, would have caused shipwreck in my life without the clearly remembered refreshment and undying certainty of this one experience.[58]

Once again, as was the case in the report at the end of chapter 2, the statement from Psalm 46:10 — "Be still, and know that I am God" — opens the doors to bliss. This woman's recognition that worry is not helpful is also a factor in her shift in viewpoint. The discovery that we do not have to let our thinking be run by whatever mortal thoughts and feelings happen to be there is the beginning of finding and living Soul dominion.

In a spontaneous realization the following writer reports on her discovery of the true meaning of "eternal life":

> This spiritual experience has haunted my life ever since April 1932. My life at that time [involved] ... the carrying of well-nigh impossible burdens of responsibility single-handed....
>
> After an exhausting day, but with nothing in it to set it apart from many others, I had thrown myself down on to my bed at night, tired out. I seemed immediately to be gathered up into such a Light of Glory (and I mean visible and vibrant Light) of which I was part, that instinctively I fell on my knees at the bedside. How long I remained there I do not know. I slept soundly afterwards.
>
> The effects of the experience remained with me, in enhanced awareness of every form of life and experience, for at least three months, during which time I possessed boundless energy and vitality. It was, for me, an entrance into the Kingdom of Heaven, and every word as spoken in the Gospels by Jesus rang true to the facts of that experience. Eternal life was seen as a quality of life, which could be received and entered into here and now.[59]

The last words of this testimony point to the central issue of Life: "here and now." Some years ago a formula came to mind that has repeatedly helped me find my Soul center. I call it the Right Now Meditation:

> There is only here and now.
> And right now,
> everything that really is, already is,
> and always has been, and always will be.
> And right now,
> everything that really isn't, already isn't,
> and never has been, and never will be.[60]

What really is is the universal and eternal quality Life of Soul's seeing. What really isn't is the mortal misconception of the material ego's seeing. We don't have to make what isn't not be, since it already isn't. In the conscious celebration of what is, the kingdom of Soul as the center and source of our being, we increasingly lose sight of the misconception and its experiences. For "I" dwell in the house of the Lord — the bliss of Soul awareness — forever.

Amen

Listen to the song of life.
Store in your memory the melody you hear.
Learn from it the lesson of harmony...

... For as the individual has voice, so has that in which the individual exists. Life itself has speech and is never silent. And its utterance is not, as you that are deaf may suppose, a cry: it is a song.[61]

The Soul is the song at the heart of each one of us. It is our own, perfect song, and it is not other than God's song. God is the Singer and man is the song.

The meaning and purpose of life on this plane is to find and live our song. The song is already singing itself and it is the truth of us before, during, and after this lifetime. There is nothing on earth that can give or take away our song. But we must love ourselves enough to seek and honor our song, or we will think ourselves apart from it, deprived and bereft.

The prince of this world will come to us declaring that we are not whole, beautiful, strong, creative, pure, innocent, and free. But the static of his voice is not stronger than the song of Life within. We will only listen harder, listen with all our hearts, and know that we can never be separated from the song that is our Soul.

Notes

1. Subsequently republished in *The Atlantic Harvest* (Boston: Little, Brown & Co., 1947), and under separate cover, with excerpts from responding letters, by Macalester Park Publishing Co., St. Paul, Minn., in the same year.

2. James Redfield, *The Celestine Prophecy* (New York: Warner Books, 1993), 44.

3. Abraham Maslow, *Toward a Psychology of Being*, 2d ed. (New York: Van Nostrand Reinhold, 1968), 7.

4. Ibid., back cover.

5. "An American Hymn," music by Lee Holdridge, Lyric by Molly Ann Leikin, copyright Zagazig Music and Arden Drive Music, 1981, 1987.

6. Joseph Campbell, *The Power of Myth* (Garden City, N.Y.: Doubleday, 1988), 120.

7. Mary Baker Eddy, *Science and Health* (Boston: First Church of Christ, Scientist, 1971), 264.

8. C. B. G., in Eddy, *Science and Health*, 668–69.

9. Quoted in *Twenty Minutes of Reality* (St. Paul: Macalester Park Publishing Co., 1947), 60–62.

10. Philip Kapleau, *Three Pillars of Zen* (Garden City, N.Y.: Anchor Press/Doubleday, 1980), 279–80.

11. Abraham Pais, *"Subtle Is the Lord...": The Science and the Life of Albert Einstein* (New York: Oxford University Press, 1982), Foreplate.

12. Richard Hughes, *A High Wind in Jamaica* (New York: New American Library, 1961), 98–101.

13. Thomas Hora, *Dialogues in Metapsychiatry* (New York: Seabury Press, 1977), 184.

14. Larry Dossey, M.D., *Recovering the Soul* (New York: Bantam Books, 1989), 1–3.

15. Joseph Campbell, *The Power of Myth* (Garden City, N.Y.: Doubleday, 1988), 222.

16. Quoted in Nona Coxhead, *The Relevance of Bliss* (New York: St. Martin's Press, 1985), 38–40.

17. Ibid., 51–52.

18. Cited in Marianne Williamson, *A Return to Love* (San Francisco: Harper-Collins, 1992), 95.

19. Elizabeth Von Arnim, *The Enchanted April* (New York: Pocket Books, 1993), 143, 288.

20. Ibid., 95, 96, and 97.

21. Thomas Hora, *The Soundless Music of Life* (Orange, Calif.: PAGL Press, 1983), 31–32.

22. Williamson, *A Return to Love,* 103.

23. Thomas Hora, *In Quest of Wholeness,* out of print, 3.

24. Ann Linthorst, *Mothering as a Spiritual Journey: Learning to Let God Nurture Your Children and You Along with Them* (New York: Crossroad Publishing Co., 1993), 137.

25. Mrs. D. E., quoted in Raynor Johnson, *Watcher on the Hills* (New York: Harper & Bros., 1959), 92–93.

26. Shunryu Suzuki, *Zen Mind, Beginner's Mind* (New York: Weatherhill, 1980), 54.

27. Marianne Williamson, *A Return to Love* (San Francisco: HarperCollins, 1992), 105.

28. Polly Berrien Berends, *Coming to Life: Traveling the Spiritual Path in Everyday Life* (San Francisco: Harper & Row, 1990), 53.

29. Ann Linthorst, *Thus Saith the Lord, Giddyap! Metapsychiatric Commentaries* (Orange, Calif.: PAGL Press, 1986), 36–77. Available from the author.

30. Allan Farber, Ph.D., Oakland, Calif.

31. James Redfield, *The Celestine Prophecy* (New York: Warner Books, 1993), 138.

32. Linthorst, *Mothering as a Spiritual Journey.*

33. Quoted in Philip Kapleau, *Zen: Dawn in the West* (Garden City, N.Y.: Anchor Press/Doubleday, 1979), 141–43.

34. From the Foreword to Doris Dufour Henty, *Addresses and Other Writings on Christian Science* (Carmel, Calif.: Mulberry Press, 1990), ix.

35. Renee Weber, *Dialogues with Scientists and Sages: The Search for Unity* (New York: Routledge & Kegan Paul, 1986), chapter 1.

36. Elizabeth von Arnim, *The Enchanted April* (New York: Pocket Books, 1993), 18–19; 66–67.

37. Quoted in "Some Illuminating Letters" in *Twenty Minutes of Reality* (St. Paul: Macalester Park Publishing Co., 1947), 41–43.

38. John Hargreaves, *As 'I' See It: A Scientifically Spiritual Perspective* (Carmel, Calif.: Mulberry Press, 1995), see chapter 4.

39. Shunryu Suzuki, *Zen Mind, Beginner's Mind* (New York: Weatherhill, 1971), 62–63, 67.

40. Nona Coxhead, *The Relevance of Bliss* (New York: St. Martin's Press, 1985), 45–46.

41. Quoted in "Some Illuminating Letters" 39–40.

42. Coxhead, *The Relevance of Bliss,* 71–72.

43. Meg Greenfield, "Politics' Sacred Lie," *Newsweek,* November 7, 1994.

44. James Redfield, *The Celestine Prophecy* (New York: Warner Books, 1993), 226, 227.

45. Cited in Hargreaves, *As 'I' See It,* 108.

46. Andras Angyal, *Neurosis and Treatment: A Holistic Theory* (New York: John Wiley & Sons, 1965), 225–26.

47. John Hargreaves, *The Christian Science Revolution in Thought* (Carmel, Calif.: Mulberry Press, 1993), 245.

48. Andy Rooney, commentary on *60 Minutes*, CBS, April 23, 1995.

49. Quoted in Richard Bucke, *Cosmic Consciousness* (New York: E. P. Dutton & Co., 1923), 327.

50. Quoted in *Twenty Minutes of Reality* (St. Paul: Macalester Park Publishing Co., 1947), 50–51.

51. Mary Baker Eddy, *Miscellaneous Writings*, in *Prose Works* (Boston: First Church of Christ, Scientist, 1953), 125.

52. John Hargreaves, *As 'I' See It: The Scientifically Spiritual Perspective* (Carmel, Calif.: Mulberry Press, 1995), see chap. 16.

53. Margaret Montague, *Twenty Minutes of Reality* (St. Paul: Macalester Park Publishing Co., 1947).

54. Mary Baker Eddy, *Science and Health* (Boston: First Church of Christ, Scientist, 1971), 247–48.

55. Germaine Greer, *The Change: Women, Aging and the Menopause* (New York: Alfred A. Knopf, 1992) 372, 377, 10.

56. Sogyal Rinpoche, *The Tibetan Book of Living and Dying* (San Francisco: HarperSanFrancisco, 1992), 260–61.

57. Quoted in Rev. Irving C. Tomlinson, *Twelve Years with Mary Baker Eddy* (Boston: The Christian Science Publishing Society, 1973), 47–48.

58. Mrs. M. E. A., in Raynor Johnson, *Watcher on the Hills* (New York: Harper & Bros., 1959), 50.

59. Ibid., 48.

60. Ann Linthorst, *Thus Saith the Lord: Giddyap! Metapsychiatric Commentaries on Human Experience and Spiritual Growth* (Orange, Calif.: PAGL Press, 1986), 42. Available only from the author.

61. From "Light on the Path." Quoted in *Twenty Minutes of Reality*, 49.